POLICE IN DEMOCRATIC SOCIETIES

SANKAR SEN

GYAN PUBLISHING HOUSE
NEW DELHI-110002

Police in Democratic Societies
(Police)

ISBN: 81-212-0655-3

Published in 2000 in India by
Gyan Publishing House
5, Ansari Road
New Delhi-110002
Phone's: 3282060, 3261060
Fax: 3285914
E-mail: gyanbook@del2.vsnl.net.2
Web Site At http.\\www.gyanbooks.com

Laser typesetting at: Gaurav Computer, New Delhi
Printed at: Mehra Offset Press, New Delhi

CONTENTS

Section-V

Section-VI

Appendix

Foreword

I am happy to have been asked to write the foreword for the book *Police in Democratic Societies*. Mr. Sankar Sen, the author, was the Diretor-General of Investigation in the National Human Rights Commission when I was working as its Chairman. These thirty-three articles had appeared separately at different times and I had read many of them. I am happy that the author and the publisher have agreed to put them together and provide excellent reading material in a book form.

In October 1993, the Commission came into existence under an ordinance. Many people were very critical openly stated that the Commission had been set up to cover up misdeeds and gross violations of human rights by the defence forces, the police and others in public offices. When the question of picking up the head of the Investigating team came up in this back ground, we became very cautious and wanted to pick up an appropriate police officer-capable, honest, hardworking-with adequate professional talent and bearing and above all a gentleman in uniform.

After about three months of search, we identified Mr. Sen. He was then Director of the National Police Academy at Hyderabad on the verge of retirement. The Commission decided to wait till he retired, got his papers cleared and in June 1994 he joined. The Chairman, three learned colleagues, a Secretary-General and the Diretor-General got set with determination to make the statute operative.

Mr. Sen perceived the requirements of his job in the right way. He soon groomed an excellent team of investigatiors. He taught them gentle behaviour, adequate grip and firmness, honestly in dealings and deft handling of every matter. Within three months visible results appeared. Investigation was the point where the Commission came close to the people and if the team worked well, the Commission became effective.

In Mr. Sen, we found an excellent combination of qualities that his job required. He understood that police power could not be exhibited in a raw form. He very well knew that in our democratic polity, it was the people who mattered; he was equally aware of the position that the common man had a low rating of the police. We soon considered Mr. Sen as a true democrat and started utilising his service even for reconciliation of disputes.

Mr. Sen, a profuse reader and writer, knows well how to project thoughts and make his views acceptable to the reader. He has covered a wide spetrum and keeping the police at the centre has operated his pen in different facets.

He believed and used to tell us that there is nothing wrong with the manpower in the manpower in the police. What was needed were direction and leadership. He has shown by this work that he was right. His writings in this book are a reassurance of what he used to say.

Mr. Sen is well-known to his readers, within and even outside the country. I am sure the reader would find the present book useful and pleasant reading. May I add, every policeman should read and perhaps re-read this book to learn that the little man on the street, is his real master! And that is what Mr. Sen's book points out.

Ranganath Misra

Preface

The book contains a number of articles dealing with various aspects of police work and problems of law-enforcement in India and other democratic countries of the world. These articles appeared at different times in national dailies and in journals in and outside the country. Thoughts and views expressed in these articles are based on my long years of exposure in law-enforcement, wide-ranging discussion with the police officers of various ranks and other functionaries of the criminal justice system and my work experience in the National Human Rights Commission. Problems of policing democratic societies are complex and varied. While maintaining peace and orderliness in the society and fighting against the forces of chaos and disruption the police will have to respect the fundamental rights of the citizens. The touchstone of good policing is concern for protection of human rights while waging a relentless battle against crime and disorder. Order is to be maintained through law, and it is not always an easy job.

In India the problems of the policing are compounded by the fact that there is constant denunciation of the police from the press and the pulpit and without properly understanding the professional and structural problems and the moral dilemmas of the police. There does exist a wall of misunderstanding between the police and the public and this alienation of the police from the society is the outcome of various factors over some of which the police have very little control.

The articles in the book cover subjects on various aspects of policing. The issue of police brutality figures in a couple of articles. This problem exists in demoratic societies to a greater or lesser degree. However, in countries like the United Kingdom and Japan where the police enjoy public confidence and regard, there are few occasions of brutal use of force by the police; but the situation is different in countries like the USA and India where the public regard for the police is poor and the instances of police violence and brutality are frequent. In a few articles I have emphasised the overriding need for depoliticising the police. It is imperative that the police must function according to the rule of law and not on the whims and dictates of others. Totalitarian states are called police states because not only the police there enjoy untrammelled authority but remain constanly vulnerable to extra-legal pressures and influence.

However, police autonomy and accountability must go side by side. This is line with the view expressed by the National Human Rights Commission in is Annual Reports and submissions before the Supreme Court that the police in a democratic society must be "low in authority and high in accountability". Some institutional mechanisms have to be devised to insulate the police from extraneous pressures and influence. Setting up of the State Security Commission as suggested by the National Police Commission, and some modifications regarding its composition and suggested by the National Human Rights Commission, require a close look. Indian Police without important structural reforms will not be able to cope with the aweome challenges of crime control and order mainteance in the new millennium. In many demoratic countries there is now emergence of civil oversight bodies to look into the serious compliants against the police. Experience of dealing with police misconduct in different countries of the world shows that exclusive reliance on police self-regulation is not sufficient. Capacity of the police to regulate itself is limited and does not carry conviction with the people. The article on the functioning of the Police Complaints Authority in the U.K. also shows how difficult it is for an external agency to thoroughly investigate into the complaints against the police and win public confidence. There is also police opposition to the formation and functioning of such bodies.

The articles dealing with the twin problems of crime control and crime investigation seek to dispel the popular notion that efficiency or inefficiency of the police is the most important factor behind increase or reduction in crime. The capacity of the police to check and control crime is much limited by the social and economic factors over which it has no control. Empirical researches in western countries demonstrate that successful crime prevention strategies must include enlistment of public support and co-operation. The police will have to evolve mechanisms for discussing crime prevention strategies with members of the community by deepening contacts and holding regular meetings. This is now happening in many democratic countries of the West. It is now recognised that the critical ingredient in crime detection is whether the public, victims and witnesses, provide promptly information to the police that help it to identify the suspects.

The articles in the book on police training contain my considered b views on the present state of police training in the country and the need for completely reorganising it. It is a crowning pity that in India though the police was the first civil service to think of systemic institutional training for its personnel, the police training institutions now are in a bad shape. Institutional facilities are minimal and there is near-total dearth of good instructors. Training institutional have become dumping grounds for incompetent and demotivated personnel of the force. The Gore Committe hit the nail on the head when it observed that the most important reason for this unhappy situation was lack of conviction about the value of training on the part of the administration including the higher ranks of the police service. However, I have always felt that the training though essential is not the only input for improving and optimising work performance and bringing about attitudinal transformation of police officers and men. Training can be effective only if the organisational climate encourages observance of precepts taught during the training.

The articles on terrorism were mostly written when terrorist violence convulsed Punjab and sent shock-waves throughout the country. However, today the scourge of terrorism has become worldwide and no foolproof remedies against this difficult and persistent feature of international violence are yet on the horizon. In an article on Punjab terrorism I have expressed the opinion that there is need for a considerate and magnanimous view in favour of the police officers who committed bonafide excesses in discharge of the thankless duties during the war against terrorism in Punjab. Without showing clemency to those responsible for acts of deliberate violence against innocent citizens, it may be possible to take a more compassionate view in cases of other whose aberrations were bonafide and not motivated. This article of mine triggered off angry protests from many a human rights activist. There are articles in the book on subjects of great human rights concern like child rape, child marriage, insufferable condition of the undertrials, violation of the human rights of the prisoners etc. Views expressed in these articles had been the outcome of my experience gathered and insights gained as the Director General of the National Human Rights Commission. These are important societal issues which have to be dealt with urgency and a sense of compassion if we are to build up a caring and humane society in the country. Further, assignment in the National Human Rights Commission gave me a unique opportunity to view some of our deep-seated societal and systemic problems from the human rights perspective and from the viewpoint of the underprivileged and vulnerable groups of the society.

I do hope that this bunch of articles will evoke interest among the academics, lawenforcement officers as well as members of the public. Policing a perplexed democratic society is a complex problem. It requires professional insight of a high order on behalf of the police officers, and particularly the police leaders, and it also needs understanding by the public of the factors that impinge on good governance and successful law-enforcement.

Dr. Sankar Sen

Section-I

1

Police Brutality in Perspective: Dirty Harry Problem

Incidents of police violence and excesses are covered prominently by newspapers everyday. Not only do the English newspapers but the language dailies also carry in banner lines stories of police highhandedness and brazen acts of atrocity. These make painful reading. Few years ago shocking incidents of the gunning down of two innocent men in Connaught Place or the brutal onslaught on Martin Massey only strengthen the popular perception of the police as a brutal outfit. One forms an impression that the police force in the country consists only of cruel, if not blood-thirsty, maniacs who relish the sight of broken skulls or blinded eyes. This boorish and brutalised image of the police is not wholly true. I have come across many committed and motivated police officers of high integrity with deep concern for the rights of the citizens. Unfortunately, in our country, very little empirical research has been done on the psychology and behavioural patterns of the police. An illuminating study on 'Violence and the Police' conducted by an American Sociologist William A Wesley, in an unnamed city of the USA did find evidence of a small number of policemen who were sadists and who frequently committed brutalities repugnant to the rest of the police force. However, the study revealed that the force also attracted men imbued with idealism—men with similar psychological profiles as doctors and ministers. The same is also true of the Indian police. There are many committed policemen in different ranks possessing a high degree of motivation which enable them to withstand the stress and strain of their dauntless job.

It is a fact that the job of the police is difficult and unbelievably thankless. It is aptly said that from on other service so much is demanded with so little recompense. Long ago, (1710) Daniel Defoe wrote: "The imposition of the office of the constable is an unsupportable hardship; it takes up so much of a man's time that his own affairs are frequently totally neglected, too often to his ruin". Difficult conditions in which the police function, the various types of hazards, including those from the scheming politicians, to which they are constantly exposed, poor working environment, appalling housing facilities, etc. have been highlighted in the reports of the National Police Commission. A study conducted by the National Productivity Council has shown that in many police stations of our country a policeman has to work 16 to 18 hours a day seven days a week. The recreation or relaxation time is short and facilities of healthy recreation are almost non-existent. It is relevant to mention here that a recent study of occupational stress and mental health of police personnel in India conducted by the National Institute of Mental Health and Neuro Sciences (NIMHANS), Bangalore, has revealed high prevalence of mental health problems among police personnel.

Stress and Strain

The emotional stress and strain of the job is further compounded by a 'pariah' feeling that haunts many policemen. The police profession, for a 'variety of reasons', is not accorded proper esteem in our country. The esteem awarded to it is grossly disproportionate to the importance of the police functions and is much lower than what is accorded to other comparable professions. Many police officers feel with a sense of righteous indignation that their achievements go unheralded and in failures are trumpeted. Large numbers of policemen every year sacrifice their lives in the line of duty and the list of such brave police officers and men whose names are read out in police commemoration parades shows a disturbingly increasing trend.

In India, unfortunately, the killing of a policeman does not produce the sense of shock and revulsion which is noticed in countries like the UK or Japan. This is because policemen are killed in the line of duty so often that emotion is blunted by familiarity. Death of a policeman is considered as an occupational hazard. Deprived of solicitude from the members of the public, policemen develop a 'self-pity syndrome', turn cynical, and view themselves as a group apart — a group that often sees the world as 'We' and 'They'. Hostility and isolation feed on one another. They develop a group solidarity which is even carried to the extent where the policemen defend even the most outrageous action of their colleagues. The comrades and service come first, justice and the public, a poor second.

A stark fact often overlooked is that police violence and brutality are correlated to the public attitude towards the police. Lowered public regard reduces police self-esteem, thereby making misuse of force by the police highly likely. On the other hand, unwarranted and unbridled use of force goes to lower public esteem for the police. Thus, an element of circularity enters the pattern. Therefore, in countries like the UK, and Japan where police enjoy public connfidence and regard, there are few occasions of brutal use of force by the police. But the situation is different in the USA, India and among other developing countries, where public regard for the police is poor and instances of police brutality and violence are frequent.

Police Force: Use and Abuse

It is also noticed that police violence and excessive use of force is restricted in societies where reserve and physical restraints are valued. This is a cultural variable. Prof. Bayley, in his 'Forces of Order—Police Behaviour in Japan and United States' says that in Japan a policeman who forebears use of force even at the risk of emotional repression is respected for doing so. By contrast, an American policeman believes that they cannot allow a challenge to go unmet. Backing down is considered cowardly.

Again, police excesses and violence often spawn from the erroneous notion of policemen to adopt short-cut, extra-legal methods to achieve results. It is true that quite often there is relentless pressure on the police, especially during difficult and turbulent times, from the political masters as well as the public to resort to unethical and illegal means and deliver rough-and-ready justice to dreaded criminals and terrorists who are cynically exploiting their rights and liberties to undermine the society which guarantees them the rights. The stark fact cannot be gainsaid that there is some amount of double-talking and double-thinking over the issue. Even enlightened members of the society expect the police to take 'strong action' not sanctioned by law against the anti-social elements who are escaping conviction and getting away scotfree because of the malfunctioning of the criminal justice system. I still recall a sensational case of double murder in Cuttack some time during 1984, when a responsible political leader suggested to me to utilise the various techniques known to a police officer to extort information from the suspects. I had to discourage him by explaining its implications. Unfortunately, many officers fail to resist such pressures and give free rein to the subordinates, who tend to lose balance and overdo it. Not only the criminals but also many innocent citizens become victims of police exceses.

Dirty Harry Problem

The struggle between the ends and the means is thus a perpetual occupational dilemma for the police. This is known in police parlance as the 'Dirty Harry Problem'. The Dirty Harry Problem traces its name from the film 'Dirty Harry' and its chief protagonist was anti-hero Inspector Harry. The heart of the problem involves juxtaposition of good ends and dirty means. Very often it is seen, and many such instances can be cited, when policemen lose their sense of moral proportion, turn cynical and allow themselves to use dirty means too readily and crudely. These practitioners of dirty means have to be pulled up. Otherwise, the legitimate and situationally justified use of force vested in the police by the society will be misused, often to the detriment of the poor and the disadvantaged. In the National Human Rights Commission (NHRC) complaints against police violence and misuse of authority come from the poor and downtrodden people who dwell on the fringes of society. Policemen inured to the use of extralegal means resort to them too readily and frequently with questionable motives. Here, I may mention that the number of deaths in police custody reported to the (NHRC) has shot up from 113 in 1995 to 201 in 1996. During the period from January to March (1997) 38 cases of death in police custody have been reported. The victims mostly belong to the poor and marginalised sections of the people.

Solutions

The answer to this festering problem is to build up a culture in the police that frowns upon misuse of force and adoption of methods not sanctioned by law. This will no doubt make policing more challenging but will also enable the police to win the support of the community in the long run. Police officers have to play the role of change-agents. They have to send clear messages down the line that extralegal methods are self-defeating and counter productive. Apart from being unlawful they are arbitrary as a process and random in their effect. External mechanisms to enforce police accountability and penalise police aberrations are necessary in a democratic society but meaningful and lasting changes in the organisation can only come from within.

2
Police Brutality Around the World

In modern democratic societies the police is vested with authority of using legitimate and situationally justified force against the citizens. This mandate given to the police to use force, if necessary, to curb and prevent violence raises the key issue that the police themselves should not abuse the authority given to it by the society to protect the rights of the citizens.

Misuse of force and authority by the police assumes varied forms in different parts of the world, as stated after the Rodney King incident in Los Angeles, by Professor David H.Bayley (2). David H.Bayley-'Police Brutality Abroad'. An article contained in the book 'Police Violence' edited by William. A Geller and, Han Toch mentions that police brutality in the United States of America has become synonymous with unjustified use of force in making an arrest. Indeed arrest-related assault and misconduct constitute one of the important complaints against the police in the United States.

Arrest related offences, however, constitute only one form of misuse of force by the police. Other forms of police brutality include torture, death in police custody, illegal detentions, implication in false cases, false arrests, custodial rape, unjustified use of force in quelling riots or dispersing mobs, shooting without justification, etc.

Amnesty International's Survey

In an international survey of torture in early 1989, Amnesty International concluded that among the democratic countries of the world police torture did not occur in Australia, Canada, Great Britain, France, Japan and Sweden. It, however, occurred in Israel and India. Torture of the Arabs and Palestinians in Israel involved in acts of terrorism is known only too well. In India allegations of use of third- degree methods used by the police hit newspaper head-lines almost everyday.

In India, complaints are received from different parts of the country containing serious allegations against the police for gross misuse of force and violation of human rights. Some of these complaints are unfounded and often sent by persons with criminal antecedents when the police close in on them. However, in many cases it has been found that there has been a gross misuse of force or callous disrespect for the rights of the citizens by the police. In a majority of the cases the victims belong to the disadvantaged and marginalised groups in the society.

Though the allegations of torture by the police are now coming to notice with increasing frequency, it is good to remember that the evil is not of recent origin. As early as in 1850, the Torture Commission (the Commission set up to investigate into the alleged cases of torture in Madras Presidency) highlighted that police torture was quite prevalent there. The Indian Police Commission (1902-03) which was set up by Lord Curzon had also written that "a serious complaint against the police is the unnecessary severity with which they often discharge their duty and unnecessary annoyances that are inflicted on the public."

In USA as early as in 1931, the National Crime Commission headed by George Wicker Ham sharply criticised the police for routine use of torture and third-degree methods. In USA in 1966 the President's Commission on "Law Enforcement and Administration of Justice" came across many incidents where the police used unnecessary force and violence.

Japan

The Japanese police have also been accused of torturing the suspects. David Bayley writes that for inquiring into the allegations of police high-handedness and torture made by the members of Tokyo Bar, two international jurists, namely Elienne Jander and Karen Parker, with the approval of the Japanese Government, probed into the charges and came to the conclusion that in Japan the police engages in "widespread physical and psychological torture, cruel, inhuman and degrading treatment."

Torture in police custody in Japan includes prolonged isolation, lack of privaey, interrupted sleep, irregular and unannounced interrogations. Though physical force was seldom applied, it was indeed threatened on many occasions. In some instances suspects were also denied access to the lawyers. In this connection it may be mentioned that under the Japanese criminal law, the suspects have to be brought before the magistrate within seventy two hours of arrest when the charges must be filed. Otherwise, the person will be set free. However, Japanese suspects can be kept in police custody instead of in prisons (judicial custody) for as long as 23 days during which police investigation may continue. This vests the Japanese police with enormous power unparalleled in modern industrial democracies to deal with the suspects. In fairness to the Japanese police, it has to be admitted that cases of torture and misuse of authority by the Japanese police are few and far between. However, some cases do take place and have prompted the Japanese Supreme Court to overturn many police cases. There is indeed enormous potential for misuse of authority.

Australia

In Australia, the Federal Government created a Royal Commission in 1988 to probe into the disproportionate number of aboriginal deaths in custody. The investigation brought about changes in management of prisons and prisoners and introduction of aboriginal lay-visitors to police lock-ups.

United Kingdom

Charges of violence have also been levelled against the police in the United Kingdom. The famous Scotland Yard too has not been immune from this criticism. Even before the Royal Commission produced its report on police behaviour in 1960, scandals began to occur. A rhino whip was discovered in a Sheffield locker and a well-organised 'firm within firm' was revealed to permeate the structure of the detectives in Metropolitan Police, reaching right up to the top including the elite Flying Squad. The 1960, the Royal Commission reported that "there was a body of evidence too substantial to disregard which in effect accused the police of stooping to the use of undesirable means of obtaining statements and occasionally giving prejudiced evidence in the courts of law."

In London, the police were also accused of excessive use of force in the death of Blair Beach, who, with others, was demonstrating against the neo-fascism and racism of the National Front in 1979. Charges of excessive use of the force surfaced during the prolonged miners strike in 1984-85. Again, during the racial riots and unrest in Brixton areas in 1981 triggered by the fascists, it was felt by many that the police tactics and methods in dealing with different ethnic groups needed improvement. This led to an official inquiry by Lord Scarman who in his critical report identified the need for improvement in police training on community and race relations.

Police Vigilantism in Latin America

Police brutality and misuse of authority is also common in many Latin American countries. Paul Chevigni in ('Edge of a Knife'—Police Violence in America: Chapter V), has mentioned in detail about the extra-legal violence and criminality indulged in by the police in some of the Latin American countries. Absence of effective internal or external mechanisms to control the police has further compounded the situation. In countries like Brazil and Argentina, police shootings are used as a means of social control. The infamous 'death squad' of Brazil in which the policemen not on duty participated was operational for a number of years. The object behind this kind of 'police vigilantism' was to ensure that notorious repeat offenders are taught a lasting lesson. A common cry that is often raised is that the criminals (often meaning the entire marginalised sections of the society) have too many rights, making the criminal justice system ineffective and a war against them has to be waged without quarters.

In this connection, it may be borne in mind that data regarding police brutality and high-handedness are available mostly from the few democratic countries of the world. Police violence is far more vicious and extensive in authoritarian countries, but very little data for it are available. Police torture is common and pervasive in non-democratic countries of the Middle East, Latin America and South East Asia. Authoritarian states are called 'Police States' because the police enjoy unlimited and unbridled authority and power. There are no counter-vailing nechanisms to restrain the police. Thus, the evidence of police brutality round the world, in the words of David Bayley, is "anecdotal and impressionistic". Data are available from just a handful of democratic countries.

A Picture of Police Brutality

Very few countries keep records at the national level of complaints made against the police. Countries like Japan, France, New-Zealand, which have centralised police systems, do not publish cases of complaints made against the police. In democratic countries like Australia, Canada, the USA Federal Governments do not collect and prepare countrywise data. Different police forces publish information about complaints as figures. However, even in democratic countries, perhaps, figures of complaints against the police do not provide the correct indication about the extent of police brutality. The nature and number of complaints vary from place to place according to the facilities for lodging complaints, attitude of the officers in taking note of the complaints, knowledge of the complainants about law and procedure and accuracy in recording thr complaints. It is a fact that many of the complaints give an exaggerated picture of the incidents. Again reliance only on substantiated complaints undercounts the amount of police brutality because the process of substantiation is manipulated and unstandardised.

Maguire and Corbett have mentioned that in the United Kingdom in 1989, only 8 per cent cases of complaints against the police were substantiated, while 24 per cent were conciliated and 44 per cent were voluntarily withdrawn. The number of complaints vary with the number of policemen and the size of the population. Hence it is necessary to have the ratio of complaints per police officer as well as complaints per citizen and then make a study.

Further, cases of misconduct of the police are trumpeted while achievements go unheralded. The Chief of the Los Angeles Police Daryl Gates was strongly criticised when, after the Rodney King beating, he said that most of his officers behave in an acceptable and professional manner. The view of the police chief, though politically maladroit, was correct. Police brutality is deplorable but some complaint against the police are inevitable and have to be viewed against the background of what they do. This is the reason why the British Police Complaints Authority in its annual reports emphasise the point that the conduct of the most of the British Police officers is beyond reproach.

There is also pressure on the police, especially in difficult and turbulent times, from the political masters and members of the public to resort to questionable and extralegal methods, particularly against the dreaded criminals, terrorists, etc. There is often public willingness to approve of police brutality. One of the problems facing the police today is societal pressure on them to resort to extralegal and extra-constitutional methods, which are self-defeating and counter-productive in the long run.

3

Policing a Democratic Society: The British Experience

Policing a democratic society means policing by consent which is not an easy job. Police in discharge of their duties face challenges even in societies where democracy has taken firm roots. This became clear to me during recent visit along with two other senior officers of the National Human Rights Commission to the United Kingdom and interaction with the officers of West Midlands Police Force. We had gone to Birmingham on an invitation to study the refined methods of interviewing of the suspects and victims by the police and the various measures taken by it to improve the quality of policing a multiracial society.

It is a fact that the police in the United Kingdom is passing through a period of transition. Winds of change (one senior police officer of West Mercia called it a gale) are blowing high and fast. Leitmotif of these new changes and developments is increasing professionalisation and civilianisation of the British police. The computer has come in a big way in all spheres of police work. It has been of immense help in storage and retrieval of information and has significantly reduced paperwork. Everyone remains glued to the computer and seeks its help in every possible means and manner for various police works and operations.

Though police is traditionally a rule-bound conservative organisation yet systematic efforts are being made to introduce management principles and techniques in police work to make the organisation less bureaucratic and bloated on the one hand and more responsive to the requirements of the people on the other. One key management change has been to reduce the number of senior posts by eliminating some intermediate ranks and increase the number of field officers so that police presence at the 'cutting-edge' level becomes more effective and visible. During a recent public opinion poll in West Midlands more than 90 per cent of the respondents expressed their appreciation of the police work and satisfaction at the quality of service provided by the West Midlands Police and about 80 per cent of the people felt that the police were polite and competent, while only about 20 per cent of the people were happy with the amount of high visibility of foot patrols. Police authorities have now decided to increase the number of men onfront-line duties and further improve the quality of their service.

Civilianisation

Another important development is the civilianisation of the police force. Out of the approximate 7000 personnel of the West Midlands Police, nearly 3000 are civilians, performing wide-ranging functions with differing status and levels of responsibility. Civilians are deployed in manual posts like cleaners and mechanics, in administrative and clerical posts in headquarters and at divisions as press officers and administrative officers and in technical posts as computer programmers and data analysts, etc. In 1966, the Tavern Report recommended the need for employing more civilians in the police with a view to releasing policemen for core police duties. This arrangement is definitely more cost-effective and builds closer links between the police and the community. In the coming years there will be more professional civilian support for the police service in Great Britain.

There is also change in another important respect. Nowadays, more qualified and bright people are joining the rank of constables. In the UK, as per the old practice, every police officer has to join in the rank of a constable and then work his way up. I met a law graduate as well as a management degree holder who have joined in constable's rank. However, for academically and technically qualified people, there is scope for accelerated promotion.

A big challenge for the police in the U.K. is how to improve its relations with different ethnic groups. There is now a felt need for the police to become more responsive to the needs of a multi-cultural and multi-racial society. The 1991 census shows that almost five per cent of Britain's populations comprises visible ethnic minorities, of them half having been born in Britain and most of the rest having lived the greater part of their lives in Britain. The 1976 Race Relations Act renders racial discrimination in the provisions of employment and services illegal. Discrimination on grounds of colour or race is banned. Following disturbances in London and other British cities in 1981, Lord Scarman's report on 'British disorders' identified the need for improvements in police training on community and race relations. Further in order to help the police in this work in each police division, there are local consultative committees. We met the members of the Sandwell (a place near Birmingham) police Consultative Committee. Members hailing from India, Pakistan snd Carribbean countries were appreciative of police efforts to promptly deal with racial incidents and related about frank and constructive exchange of views with police officers during meeting of the consultative committees. Officers of the community services of West Midlands police have been advised to keep close contact with members of the committee and respond positively to suggestions and well-funde criticisms. Police officers have been further advised to look on consultative committees as valuable opportunities to influence important members of the community and project the police point of view properly.

Statistics of racial incidents of Sandwell Division disclosed that as many as 147 racial incidents were roported in sandwell division in 1996. This marks a 58 per cent increase on 1995. The incidents include racial harassment, racial graffiti, assault, robbery, etc. Robin Oakely, a well-known consultant specialising in race relations and equal opportunities, writes that "racial discrimination continues to be a frequent occurrence, though invisible to those who suffer it because it happens in indirect ways." National attitude surveys indicate that at least one-third of Britons are willing to admit that they are racially prejudiced to some degree.

Lay Visiting Scheme

However, it was heartening to note that senior police officers are seriously concerned over this problem in the force and do not shy away from taking stringent measures against the defaulters and sending correct signals down the line. Some clear and concrete steps have been taken to ensure proper code of practice by the police in respect search, detention and treatment of persons in police custody. The Police and Criminal Evidence Act I, 1984, lays down codes of practice to be followed by the police. They provide clear and workable guidelines for the police balanced by strong safeguards for the public. Random checks by persons other than police officers on the interrogation and detention of. suspects in police stations have now been introduced in the form of 'Lay Visiting Scheme'. Under the scheme lay visitors who are representatives from local organisations make unscheduled and unannounced visits to the police stations to monitor the condition of the individuals arrested by the police. However, instances of custodial violence by the police are few and far between.

One also notices that within a hierarchical organisation like the police subordinate officers and men are treated with dignity and respect which one often misses in the Indian police. A chief superintendent in the headquarters office of West Midlands Police while taking me round the office building did not feel it proper to step inside an Inspector's room because the latter was busy in his work. An Inspector of Police could participate freely in discussions even with an Assistant Chief Constable and express his views frankly and forcefully.

Indeed, police in Great Britain enjoys public support and approval which is unparalleled in the experience of any other country. The Royal Commission as a part of its enquiry mounted a large scale national survey on police-public relations. The survey had shown an "overwhelming vote of confidence in the police .... Not less than 83 per cent of those interviewed professed great respect for the police" (Royal Commission on the Police 1962, pp. 102-103). But those halcyon days seem to be over. The police in Britain is now facing momentous challenges in rising crime and public disorder and apparent police inability to effectively deal with it. Accusations of sex and race discrimination have started diminishing public confidence in the police. The police feel under attack as never before. Leaders of the force have understood the problems and introduced a number of measures to deal with it. They have sought to improve working procedures and become more responsive to the public through various kinds of consultation. The government has also launched measures to make policing more businesslike. The Sheehy Enquiry recommended that all police officers be appointed on short-term contracts and subjected to performance-related pay (PRP).

However, the basic reason behind this gathering storm against the police lies elsewhere. In a post modern society where there is no central reference point and consumerism has become the motivating force of action, there is growing disregard for the police which stands for order and harmony. Further, the police have been able to operate for long with limited powers and in limited numbers because the family and community standards were such that law was enforced informally. Decline in the influence of the family and other sociological changes have now brought unforeseen pressures on the police. Policing a perplexed society has become a delicate and difficult job.

4
Lynch Killing: An Ominous Trend

Recently while inaugurating a Community Policing Project at Durgapur, the Chief Minister of West Bengal, Shri Jyoti Basu, blamed the police for the growing tendency among the people to take law in their own hands. Incidents of lynching the criminals or miscreants have sharply increased all over the country. People no longer repose faith in the criminal justice system of the country which has become cumbrous, slow-moving and effete, but have started believing in 'vigilantism'—taking laws in their own hands and delivering instant justice. This no doubt augurs ill for law-enforcement and order-maintenance in the country.

Police alertness can, of course, prevent some cases of lynching of criminals, but the reason for this growing phenomenon lies elsewhere. One must critically analyse the reasons and go into the heart of the matter. And then perhaps some suitable corrective strategies can be worked out. Mere police-bashing will not help. It will only further alienate the police from the public and erode its credibility.

Crime Statistics

Today the country is witnessing a surge in crime and lawlessness. Official crime statistics, yardsticks for measuring law and order situation in the state, do not reveal the sombre ground realities. In the year 1992 about 52 lakhs cognisable crime were reported in the country, marking an increase of 2.5 per cent over the figures of the previous year. It is, however, well-known to all senior police officers that there is a massive burking of crime. Even by a very conservative estimate, actual incidence of crime is four to five times more than what is reported. Large number of cases also go unregistered. One of the frequent complaints against the police before the NHRC is non-registration of cases, particularly in rural areas. This malpractice of non-registration arises from several reasons.

Among all such reasons the most important one, as the National Police Commission has so forcefully highlighted in its report, is the anxiety of the political executive in the State Government to keep the recorded crime figures low so as to claim before the State Legislature, the public and the press that the crime is well-controlled and is even going down as a result of efficient police administration under their charge.

Victimization Survey

In many developed countries like Great Britain, USA, Canada, Netherlands, USA, now apart from crime reviews, crime victimization survey is done to get a clear idea of the magnitude and impact of crime. Crime reviews are normally based on information collected by the police. Criminal victimization survey has now changed the situation and created the second source of information and become a regular feature of crime statistics. The NHRC is now planning to sponsor a crime victimization survey by a recognised study group in a metropolitan city. This will be one of the pioneering victimization surveys in the country and will provide a rich harvest of useful victimological data. However, even the suppressed crime figures of the country cannot conceal the glaring fact that in the year 1992 dacoity recorded an increase of 10.5 per cent, murder 23.2 per cent over the quinquennial average. Rape increased 22.2 per cent over q.a. and 12.5 per cent over 1991. The degree of violence used by the offenders in the commission of crimes has also sharply increased due to frequent use of fire-arms and explosives.

Against this backdrop of rising crimes and crescendo of violence due to the operation of various crimogenic factors, it is seen that the present criminal justice system is offering no credible deterrence. The criminals have come to realise that crime pays and gains of crime outweigh its risks. Jeremy Bentham, well-known philosopher-cum-penologist, had unerringly observed that the real deterrent against crime is "the certainty and not the severity of punishment."

Adversarial Pattern

The administration of criminal justice in India follows the Anglo-Saxen Adversarial pattern with greater stress on proof than on truth. In order to produce the desired impact the different segments of the criminal justice system—the police, courts and correctional institutions, must function in harmony and cohesion. Unfortunately, however, the three segments of the criminal justice system instead of inter-acting tend to counter-act one another. The result is that experienced professional criminals have come to know that in the present system of trial and investigations they have very good chances of escaping punishment altogether.

This is also borne out by hard facts and cold statistics. According to the figures compiled by the National Crime Records Bureau (Crime in India, 1992) altogether 42,74,361 IPC cases came up for trial during the year 1992 including cases from the previous years. Only 20 per cent of the cases could be disposed of, leaving behind 80 per cent of the cases (33,97,961 cases) pending disposal at the end of the year. Again percentage of conviction in respect of serious crimes has sharply plummeted during the year 1992. Out of total 19,241 murder cases, conviction was only in 8,041 cases. Out of 5,867 cases of rape, conviction was in respect of 1981 cases only. These are all-India figures. I know that in some states seriously ravaged by crimes, conviction figures in respect of heinous offences has gone below 12 per cent. This is a frightening situation. The sieving process of the criminal justice system is functioning more in favour of the offender. Once a criminal escapes punishment, he becomes more daring and develops the notion that crime pays. One has to remember the perspicacious observation of Lord Devlin that when a "criminal goes free, it is as much a failure of abstract justice as when an innocent man is convicted".

Today malfunctioning of the criminal justice system stems mainly from the incapability of the police to honestly and efficiently investigate criminal cases and apply crime control measures, and abnormal delay in disposal of cases by the courts of law. Because of multifarious commitments and extraneous pressure, the police officers have no time for thorough investigation of cases. A sample survey done by the National Police Commission in six States of the country had revealed that an investigating officer is able to devote only 37 per cent of his time in investigational work while the rest of his time is taken up by other duties like VIP Bandobust, petition enquiries, court attendance, etc. Indeed crime prevention and detection work of the police has been relegated to the background. The NHRC has now decided to press the government to accept the salient recommendations of the National Police Commission and initiate steps for separation of the law and order from the investigation staff of the police. A certain number of officers has to be ear-marked only for investigation of cases and should not be summoned for law and order and other miscellaneous duties. This, of course, will need substantial augmentation of the strength of police staff at Thana level.

Delay in disposal of cases in law courts is another cancerous evil eating into the vitals of the criminal justice system which, to be effective and credible, must function with speed. Unfortunately, in various courts of the country there is a staggering number of cases pending at various stages of adjudication. According to a study done by the Bureau of Police Research and Development, the number of cases pending in 1987 in different High Courts for more than 5 years exceeded 35 thousand. Now the position has further worsened. As a result, the jails are crowded to asphyxiation by the undertrials. The NHRC members and officers visiting different jails find to their dismay that more than 80 per cent of the prisoners are undertrials. I, myself have seen young under trials languishing in jails over a number of years along with hardened criminals. Foreigners involved in Narcotic Drugs and Psychotropic Substances (NDPS) Act cases have bitterly complained before me in Central Prisons at Madurai, Madras and Tihar that cases against them are dragging on for more than five to six years and they do not know when their ordeal will come to an end. I did feel that their angry and vitriolic outbursts against the slow pace of trial of the cases were not without substance.

Therefore, it is no wonder that people have started thinking of adopting other than legal measures to settle their complaints and grievances. Very often it takes the from of asking police to adopt illegal and coercive measures to firmly deal with hardened criminals, terrorists, etc. who are taking fullest advantage of our effete criminal justice system. Large-scale lawlessness and disorder in the country sometimes prompt even well-intentioned citizens actuated by negative emotions, fear and anger to advocate draconian means. It is important to remember that abuses of authority by police can flourish not only because of official negligence or acquiescence but because, rightly or wrongly, many people approve of it as a necessary and unpleasant task. Such conditions do impose considerable moral burden on conscientious police officials whose task of checking drift of this kind is of paramount importance.

This question of public expectation and pressure on the police is posed before me even by many senior police officers when I interact with them during my tours of duty. I repeat before them what as the Director of the National Police Academy I always used to tell the IPS probationers that the police are accountable to law and have to function within its four corners. They have no authority to take laws in their own hands and function as investigators as well as executioners. There is no scope for counter-violence under the Indian Penal Code.

I know of a case where the officer-in-charge of a police station got rid of two notorious criminals of his jurisdiction by inciting mobs to lynch them. This kind of perversity is now displayed by many police officers. Lynch mobs, as psychologists point out, armour themselves with a sense of their retributive righteousness. They also mean to exert social control by exemplary doses of terror on the conceit that violence is the only language the victims understand. Each atrocity has its own circumstances, its own atmosphere and triggers. The first American vigilantes called themselves the "regulators" because they viewed their action as restoring balance to a situation that was out of control.

Lynch killings, however, clearly betoken people's lack of faith in the criminal justice administration. They are ominous warning signals. Instead of only blaming the police, the political masters should seriously think of ways and means to revitalise the near-collapsing criminal justice system. The National Police Commission correctly recommended the appointment of a Criminal Justice Commission for the country which will look into all the sub-systems integratedly instead of appointing a Police Commission, Prison Reforms Commission or asking the Law Commission to go into the matters of judiciary alone. The criminal justice system is to be revamped and made a more meaningful instrument for delivery of justice to all sections of the people.

According to demographic projections, the population of the country will reach one billion mark by the end of the century. Increase of population density means aggravation of interpersonal tensions and higher degree of anonymity, both of which are crimogenic. The country is going to face in the coming years a rising tide of crime and lawlessness with a criminal justice machinery ill-equipped to face the onslaught. Political leaders and enlightened citizens must pause and ponder over it.

5
Soaring Crime in the Capital

The incidents of double murders in quick succession at Saket in New Delhi are very disturbing. The public is bound to feel scared and worried. The victims were elderly couplesi; in other words soft and easy targets for the cold-blooded criminals. Inevitably, there is sharp criticism of the police from the media and public for its inefficiency and negligence.

The Press reports show that the Lt.-Governor of Delhi also has joined the chorus of criticism against the police. Consequently, two police officers, one ACP an and inspector have been transferred and another sub-inspector have been suspended and the personnel of the paramilitary forces have been drafted for intensifying patrolling. However, the hard fact has to be faced that these panic measures will not help in controlling escalation of violent crime, though they may produce some shock effects on Delhi Police ranks and may convey a message to the agitated members of the public that police authorities will not spare their officers if they fail to control crime. These shock therapies, one is afraid, will not improve matters.

Political Interference

It is true that selection of officers, and particularly, the SHOs, have to be done very carefully keeping in mind their professional ability and competence and knowledge of the locality. Selection has to be done only by the police chief because they are his commanders in the field in the battle against crime and lawlessness. Unfortunately, selection is often done by powers that be on considerations other than merit and the police chief, if he wants to remain in the saddle, has to kow tow to the wishes of the political masters. I know of a chief minister of the state who, in an open conference of the senior police officers, without the slightest hesitation said that an officer in charge, if he wants to continue in the police station, has to keep the MLA of the ruling party in good humour. Naturally SHOs remain busy in humouring local politicians. rather than working out effective crime control strategies. Many of these yes-men also lack in professionalism, often indulge in questionable tactics and become unamenable to control by their senior officers.

Further, police efficiency or inefficiency, as path-breaking criminological studies have shown, is not going to the sole decisive factor in the control of crime. Crime results from many factors interwoven with one another. The Commission on "Enforcement of Law and Administration of Justice" appointed by President Lyndon Johnson in America very aptly said in its report that the "community's most enduring protection against crime is to cure the ills and right the wrongs that tempt men to harm their neighbours."

Crime Control in America

In USA, when soaring crime was a major problem facing the nation in the seventies, the criminologist James P. Wilson pointed out that additional police presence is not the real answer. It will have only marginal impact on crime control. The post-war crime prone juvenile groups following baby booms were responsible for a large number of crimes and escalation of crime cannot be reversed until they grow older. Today, not only in New York (though this is very much bruited), but in different cities of America, there is a perceptible fall in crimes, and particularly violent crimes, and one of the important factors behind it is that with American society becoming an aged society, there is decline in the number of crime-prone juvenile segments of the population. The city of New York has experienced an unprecedented decrease in crime in the year 1997. Crime has come down by 45 per cent in New York and for this, the mayor of the city Rudolph Guliani and the officers and men of New York police feel very proud.

Another fact to be borne in mind is that real reduction of crime is possible only when there is fair and vigorous law enforcement, decisive prosecution and realistic punishment of the criminals. For achieving this end, the different components of the criminal justice system must function in a spirit of cohesion and not come in each other's way to help in the proliferation of crime. Today, owing to the malfunctioning of our criminal justice system, the criminals have become aware that the crime pays and the gains of crime are more than the risks of crime. The well-known ex-Commissioner of London Metropolitan Police, Sir Robert Mark, pointed out that in the UK, a professional robber and burglar has 6 out of 10 chances of escaping arrest, and when he is caught he has 4 out of 10 chances of being acquitted. The odds are in his favour in India. The long-term effect of this is calamitous. Penal reformers like Bentham and

Rommilly down to Lord Gardiner have advocated that the control of crime lies in making punishment more certain rather than more severe. It is neither brutality nor severity, but certainty that makes punishment an effective deterrent.

The reasons for soaring crimes in Delhi are many:population explosion, unplanned urbanisation, large-scale movement of migrant population, growth of slums with appalling squalor and poverty, etc. There is also alienation of the police from the community. The public is substantially unwilling to volunteer assistance in the form of information to the police and this unwillingness indicates a powerful avoidance syndrome at work. The ratio of population per policeman in India is 1300 people and there are only 13 policemen per hundred square miles of an area. Any crime control measure will not be successful unless the members of the public are willing to come forward and help the police with valuable information. And this, the citizens will do only when they are convinced that the police wants to help them.

Building trust will not happen overnight; it will require serious confidence-building ongoing effort. For this, the police must not confine itself to the narrow role of "thief takers". Social circumstances throughout the world in its developed and less developed portions require the police to give adequate attention to the various non-enforcement tasks like providing first aid, legal advice, counsel to the juveniles, suggestions for protection of home and business. The police must give adequate attention to this non-enforcement aspects of their work. If they fail to do so and concentrate solely on enforcement, they will hamper their ability to deal with the circumstances that give rise to crime.

In this connection, it may further be mentioned that recent research findings on policing have challenged many prevailing police practices and beliefs. A research study on Kansas City Preventive Patrol Experiment done by Police Foundation of Washington found that randomised patrolling had a limited impact on crime or citizens attitude and in most cases rapid response by the police did not help to solve the crimes. The crime sample that was analysed indicated that almost two-thirds of the crimes were not reported quickly enough for rapid response to be effective. It was found that in respect of a large number of crimes, the time taken by the public to report to the police was the primary determinant of the eventual outcome.

Deployment of the paramilitary forces for patrolling and keeping surveillance over the bad characters is some sort of a knee-jerk reaction. This kind of deployment of personnel without proper knowledge of the local conditions will not deter professional criminals from committing crimes. And these professional career criminals, as Marvin Wolfgang's study has shown, are responsible for most of the serious crimes. They have to be identified and kept out of the streets. This requires professional policing and effective functioning of the other segments of the criminal justice system. There are no quick-fix strategies or solutions.

6
Bomb Blasts in Delhi

The series of bomb blasts in Delhi are bound to scare the common citizens. The powerful explosion in front of the police headquarters which occurred on 9th January 1998, is a definite challenge by the terrorists and their mentors to the State administration and a chilling message to the citizens that the former can defy the administration and carry on their violent operations with impunity. In these bomb blasts, occurring in different parts of the capital a number of people have been killed and injured. The object of the terrorists is to disorient segments of the population by showing that the government is unable to provide security and protection to the citizens and thus perform one of its basic functions. This is the reason why terrorism is called 'violence for effect'. It has to be borne in mind that the violence unleashed by the terrorists is unpredictable. It can occur at any time and at any place. Studies of the victims of the air raids during the Second World War have shown that extreme helplessness caused by the unpredictability of the danger produces acute anxiety among the people and shakes the belief "it would not happen to me". This psychologically damaging factor is amenable to manipulation by the terrorists.

For countering the terrorist operations in the capital, a mere change of guard of the Delhi Police will be of little avail. Handing over the investigation to the CBI or setting up monitoring cells under retired police officers are not perhaps appropriate strategies, but hurried responses to a grave challenge. They may have the unintended effect of further sapping the confidence and credibility of the Delhi Police.

Counter Measures

For working out counter measures, it has to be borne in mind that the first and foremost job in any counter-terrorist operation is proper and adequate collection and dissemination of intelligence. Intelligence basically means evaluated information of things that should be known in advance before initiating a course of action. However, this intelligence collection regarding terrorist operations is not an easy job. It requires very careful planning and cannot be organised as and when necessary. Different modus operandi of the terrorist groups and the random nature of their attacks make it difficult to get reliable advance warning to terrorist action. There are few early warning indicators (EWI).

Therefore covert human intelligence is the most useful source of information about the terrorists. Very often this is the only information one has to rely on. However, raising a 'source or agent in place' and handling him successfully is a slow and laborious process and requires careful preparation. Again, terrorist groups are normally divided into several small subgroups and penetration into one group may not throw light into the activities of other groups. Many terrorist groups also devise elaborate anti-infiltration procedures and ruthlessly weed out informers from their ranks. Even in countries like the UK where intelligence agencies are well organised, and the area to be covered is not very large, great difficulties have been experienced in receiving correct and adequate intelligence regarding operations of the terrorists in the areas of Northern Ireland.

For investigation into these cases of bomb blasts and apprehending the culprits there should be a special cell of Delhi Police. The local police with their ears to the ground can glean more information about the terrorists than any other outfit. This special cell must consist of capable and motivated officers who know their job. There must be full coordination between the cell and other related agencies like the RAW, the IB, the State CID and the Military Intelligence, so that there is exchange and sharing of information about the movement, methods and plans of the terrorists all over the country. Further, there is need for a centralised intelligence data computerisation which can swiftly provide information at all levels. In Western Europe, after the assassination of the then Italian Premier Aldo Moro, counter-terrorists network of the police and the security forces for the European Common Market countries has been instituted which shares knowledge and experience, including access to millions of items of information on computers on the life histories, habits and other details of the known terrorists from all over the world. This pooling of information has been of immense help in combating terrorism. In Frances, during the regime of General Charles De Gaulle. the secret service was able to penetrate into the council of the terrorists and through timely warnings foiled assassination attempts and saved the General's life on a number of occasions.

Escalation Trends Analysis

The security experts also use a techniques called the "escalation trend analysis". An analysis of the sequence of acts and the gradual escalation of violence by the terrorist groups provides predictors for their future targets and means of attack. Such an analysis also helps the security forces to tailor specific counter measures to meet such contingencies.

Ultimately, for effectively combating terrorism public support and cooperation are essential. During the bomb blasts in Mumbai, the terrorists planted bombs in as many as thirteen places and subsequently vanished. The bombs were detonated by pre-set timers. Today, sophisticated timers allow a bomb to go off even after a year. Hence, operations of the terrorist groups can be combated by obtaining precise information from the members of the public. The key to success in any anti-terrorist campaign in a democracy is a sensitized public, aware of terrorist goals and tactics and fully supportive of the needed countermeasures by the government. There is need for all-out vigilance. Deterrence works on the terrorists as it does on anyone else. Contrary to public notion, cases of suicidal terrorism are rare. Terrorist groups will start breaking up when they will find it difficult to commit terrorist acts and escape unpunished.

Here, there should be a note of caution. There are reasons to apprehend that these bomb blasts may be forerunners of greater terrorist violence in the coming days. The terrorists can even resort to chemical and other high-technology weapons that can cause heavy destruction and devastation. Some of the terrorist groups are doing precisely this in other parts of the world. Hence, emergency countermeasures and contingency plans have to be worked out at various governmental and non-governmental levels to deal with this kind of danger in time.

7
Illusions about Crime Control

There is sharp criticism of the Delhi Police from various quarters because of its failure to arrest the upsurge of crime in the capital. Indeed statistics show that there has been a marked increase in heinous crimes like murder, robbery, rape, etc., in the capital during the last few months. No doubt it is the responsibility of the police to prevent and detect crime. Prevention and detection of crime constitute the core functions of the police. The primary object of an efficient police, emphasised Charles Rowan and Richard Mayne, the first two Commissioners of Sir Robert Peel's Metropolitan Police, is "prevention of crime, the next that of detection and punishment of the offenders if the crime is committed ...... To this great end, every effort of the police is directed."

The fact, however, is to be kept in mind that for rise in crime the police alone are not responsible. The popular and prevalent notion which is also shared by the political masters is that efficiency or inefficiency of the police alone is the decisive factor behind increase or reduction of crime. This is an illusion and the sooner it is given up the better. The capacity of the police to control crime is limited. Crime results from many factors at work inextricably interwoven with one another. Efforts of the police alone to control crime will meet with limited success unless there is a multi-pronged attack on behalf of the society to deal with the real causes of crime like poverty, unemployment, ignorance, disintegration of the family, etc.

The hard fact has to be faced that not only in Delhi, but also in different parts of the country, crime is bound to increase quantitatively with the growth of population, urbanisation, economic development and breakdown of traditional institutions. Today the population of the country is almost reaching the one billion figure. Increase of population density means aggravation of intrapersonal tensions and higher degree of anonymity both of which are crimogenic. Further, various developmental activities have set off in their train forces inexorably causing an increase in crime and lawlessness.

Crime Control

Control of crime is easier in an autocratic country where rough-and-ready methods of dealing with the criminals are adopted without and problem. In some of the countries in the Middle-East because of draconian law enforcement crime is not a problem. But in a democratic society such methods like chopping off the hands of the criminals for committing crimes like theft cannot be adopted. Modern industrial democratic societies are today haunted by the spectre of rising crime. In the affluent countries of west, crime is increasing at a much faster rate than the growth of population. The most disquieting feature of the crime situation in many of the affluent countries is that the majority of the crimes are committed by young persons and children who constitute the most crime-prone sections of the population. It is interesting to note in this connection that growth of crime in post-war Britain and development of social security took place simultaneously, suggesting that classical theories relating to crime and poverty are no longer valid.

From the statistics furnished in NCRB publication 'Crime in India —1996', it is seen that total crime per lakh of population in India in 1993 was 604 whereas in Japan it was 1509, 10,954 in Canada and in England 5,128. Statistics, however, do not reveal the correct picture of the crime situation in a society. The reported crime in Indian context is barely one-fourth of the actual incidence. Nevertheless, the highly concealed crime figures also show a disturbing increase in violent crimes such as rape, dacoity, murder, etc. Such crimes recorded an increase of 31.3 per cent during the decade 1985-1995.

In this connection it can be further mentioned that in Western countries, there is now a debate over crime statistics. Criminologists are relying more upon victimisation surveys than on the reports of crimes "known to police". Victimisation survey has become a regular feature of crime statistics in the United States. Such surveys also provide useful data on why victims do not report crimes, yielding valuable insights into public attitudes and behaviours. Many criminologists regard the victimisation survey as more reliable than crimes reported to the police.

Real reduction of crime can be worked out only when there is fair and vigorous law-enforcement, prompt and decisive prosecution and realistic punishment of the criminals. For achieving this end different components of the criminal justice system must function in a spirit of harmony and cohesion and not come in each other's way and help in the proliferation of crime. Today the criminals have become aware of the limitations of the police and the system of criminal justice. They have come to know that crime can be highly profitable and rewarding. The well-known ex-Commissioner of London Metropolitan Police, Sir Robert Mark, aptly pointed out in his book *Policing a Perplexed Society*, in UK a professional robber and burglar has 6 out of 10 chances of escaping arrest, and when he is caught he has 4 out of 10 chances of acquittal. The odds are more in his favour in India where the professional criminals backed by resourceful patrons are increasingly able to get the better of the slow-moving criminal justice system. When a criminal goes scotfree, says Lord Devlin, it is as much "a failure of abstract justice as when an innocent man is convicted".

Criminal Justice System

Again, the criminal justice system in order to be effective must function with speed. Unfortunately, in different courts of the country a staggering number of cases are pending at various stages of adjudication. The Supreme Court has now taken commendable steps in reducing its arrears. The situation in the High Courts and District Courts remains unimproved.

Further, acquittal figures in criminal cases are mounting. It may be mentioned in this connection that in the past, there was regular practice of the police prosecutors to maintain close and constant relationship with the investigating officers. At present with a separate and independent prosecuting agency this is no longer the case. The prosecution staff blame the investigating officers for poor quality of investigation, resulting in acquittal, while the investigating officers condemn the prosecutors for the lack of interest in the proper presentation of cases in the court. Mutual recrimination has replaced cooperation. The upshot is that the rate of conviction, particularly in respect of heinous offences, has dropped sharply. The conviction rate, i.e., the ratio of the cases convicted to the total cases in courts was barely 42 per cent in 1995. It is true that lapses and loopholes in investigation play an important part in the acquittal of cases and this is further compounded by poor and listless prosecution. The long-term effect of this decline in the rate of conviction on crime control and order-maintenance is going to be calamitous. Penal reformers like Bentham and Romlilly down to Lord Gardiner have advocated that the control of crime lies in making punishment more certain rather than more severe. It is neither brutality or severity but certainty that makes punishment an effective deterrent.

Marvin Wolfgang's famous study of career criminals has shown that most of the serious crimes are committed by the chronic delinquents and these career criminals or 'chronic recidivists' have to be identified and kept out of streets. There should be selective incapacitation—long prison term for career criminals whose life is crime.

For improving the quality of investigation stricter supervision by the senior officers is necessary. Many investigations are botched up by field officers out of corrupt motives. But there are also genuine constraints of the police. Today police officers are overburdened with numerous miscellaneous commitments and do not have adequate time for proper investigation of cases. The National Police Commission pointed out after a study of the six States of the country that an investigation officer is able to devote only 37 per cent of his time in investigational work while the rest of time is taken up by other duties connected with the maintenance of public order, petitions and enquiries, VIP *bandobast* and court attendance. The result is perfunctory investigation of cases. Hence, separation of law and order and investigation staff is absolutely necessary. It is also to be seen that police investigation is insulated from external pulls and pressures. This point has been reiterated by the National Human Rights Commission in its submission before the Supreme Court in a writ petition filed by a retired Director-General of Police pressing the Central Government for quick implementation of the recommendations of the National Police Commission.

Investigational Work

Further, the investigational case-load of the officers is also very heavy. Investigation is a difficult, strenuous, and down-to-earth job and it is not possible for a police sub-inspector to investigate more than 75 cases a year, (a yardstick fixed by the Conference of Inspectors-General of Police and endorsed in the report of the Delhi Police Commission) with a modicum of efficiency. But the investigating officers have to investigate many more cases in addition to their various duties. Again officers are posted in important police stations on political considerations. In many of the States, SPs and even the Director-General of Police have very little say in the transfer and posting of police station officers. Many of these officers, owing to the political patronage they enjoy know that the superior officers will not be able to take them to task even if investigation is not done properly. Hence they become irresponsible and careless.

There is also over-proliferation of laws in the country. When laws are passed, framers of new laws pay little attention to the problems of enforcement and spend more time in debating the moral and abstract implications of such a legislation. Fire departments advise urban planners, architects and builders about conditions that increase the risk of fire. Health experts do the same when industrial plants are located, mining undertaken and building codes enacted, yet it is a paradox that the police are hardly consulted about whether government policies may have an impact on social processes in ways that can increase crime.

Another prevalent illusion is that crime control will be easier and detection will improve if the police rely on scientific methods of investigation. While the need for forensic science in the detection of offences cannot be overstressed, the fact has to be borne in mind that even in countries like the USA with extensive facilities of forensic science laboratories (there are more than 200 such laboratories in the USA) not more than 5 per cent of cognizable crime provide materials which can be sent to the forensic laboratories for examination. In India also not in many cases materials can be sent to forensic science laboratories. This does not minimise the importance of forensic science laboratories as many important cases of murder, rape, fraud, will come in the limited category of 4 per cent where forensic help will be important but for the remaining cases the police will have to rely upon the support and the cooperation of the members of the public.

Intelligence about crime and criminals is sine qua non for the success of investigation. This depends upon the readiness of the public to assist the police. Quick police response whenever a crime occurs, is important, but it has been significantly influenced by the speed of the police to report the incident has been crucial.

8
Torture in Police Custody

Torture has been defined and dealt with in a detailed manner in the Convention against Torture and other Cruel, Inhuman and Degrading treatment or punishment, 1984. Article-1 of the Convention defines torture as follows:

"For the purpose of this convention, the term 'torture' means any act by which severe pain or suffering, whether physical or mental, is intentionally inflicted on a person for such purposes as obtaining from him or a third person information or a confession, punishing him for an act he or a third person has committed or is suspected of having committed, or intimidating or coercing him or a third person, or for any kind, or for any reason based on discrimination when such pain or suffering is inflicted by or at the instigation of or with the consent or acquiescence of a public official or other person acting in an official capacity. It does not include pain or suffering arising only from, inherent in or incidental to lawful sanctions."

Though in India, allegations of custodial torture by the police are coming to notice with an increasing frequency, it will be good to remember that the evil is not of recent origin. The commission for investigation of alleged cases of torture in Madras Presidency (commonly referred to as the Torture Commission), in its report (1850) highlighted that police torture was quite prevalent in the then Madras Presidency. The Indian Police Commission appointed by Lord Curzon (1902-3) had also written that "the most serious complaint against the police is the unnecessary severity with which they often discharge their duty and the unnecessary annoyances they inflict upon the public". The National Police Commission also elaborately analysed the evils of custodial rape and violence and suggested a number of corrective measures.

In this connection, it is worthwhile to remember that excessive use of force by the police against persons in custody is not peculiar to

India alone. Such allegations against the police are also levelled, though that should not give room for consolation or complacency, against the police forces of advanced democratic countries. As early as in 1931, the National Crime Commission headed by George Wickershan in the United States sharply criticized the police department for routine use of torture and other third degree methods. In 1966, the President's Commission on Law Enforcement and Administration of Justice came across several incidents in which the police used unnecessary force and violence. Recent Amnesty International's Publication "United States of America—Rights for All" describes and condemns the wide-spread and persistent problem of police brutality across the USA. It says that the 'overwhelming majority of victims in many areas are members of racial and ethnic minorities while most police departments remain predominantly white' (p 18, Chapter 3).

Use of torture as a tool in policing and administration of criminal justice has been prevalent in India since ancient times. Kautilya's *Arthashastra* permitted use of torture against the spies in order to extract confession. During the Muslim rule, brutal punishment such as caning, flogging, amputation of limbs, stoning to death were meted out to the criminals. British administration took initially steps against torture and use of third degree methods. The Indian Penal Code (1862) and Indian Evidence Act (1871) contained clear provisions against torture. Sections 330 and 331 of IPC make punishable the offence of voluntarily causing grievous hurt to extract confession or compel restoration of property. Section 348 of the IPC makes punishable the act of wrongfully confining any person for the purpose of getting a confession or extracting any information. Sections 25 and 26 of the Indian Evidence Act make confession of guilt to the police officers inadmissible in evidence. Article 22 (1) of the Indian Constitution and Section 76 of the Criminal Procedure Code lay down that a person should be produced before a Magistrate within 24 hours after arrest. Section 29 of the Police Act, 1861 states that every police officer who will offer "unwarrantable personal violence to any person in his custody, shall be liable on conviction before a Magistrate to a penalty not exceeding 3 months pay or imprisonment with or without hard labour upto 3 months."

In this connection, it may be mentioned that the UN General Assembly in November, 1979 adopted a resolution prescribing a Code of Conduct for Law Enforcement Officers. Article 5 of the Code lays down "No Law Enforcement officer may inflict, instigate or tolerate any act of torture or cruel, inhuman or degrading treatment or punishment nor may any law enforcement official invoke unfair orders or exceptional circumstances such as a state of war or threat of war, a threat to national security or any other public emergency as a justification of torture". Under article 3 of the Code of Conduct, the principle of proportionality of force is underlined. In India, the Ministry of Home Affairs has also circulated a Code of Conduct for the police. The Code of Conduct enjoins the police to respect and uphold the rights of the citizens guaranteed by the Constitution.

Initiatives of the National Human Rights Commission

The National Human Rights Commission (NHRC), since its inception, has looked upon Custodial Violence as the most outrageous violation of human rights, in December 14, 1993, the commission issued instruction to the Chief Secretaries of all States asking them to direct all District Magistrates and Superintendents of Police to report any instance of custodial death or rape to the Commission within 24 hours of occurrence. Failure to send such reports, it was made clear, would lead to a presumption by the commission that an effort was being made to suppress the facts.

NHRC now receives reports of death in police and jail custody from all over the country. During the year 1995-96, 136 deaths were reported in police custody and 308 in jail custody. In the year 1996-97, however, figures reported to the commission were 188 deaths in police custody and 700 deaths in jail custody. The commission was also informed that during the year 1996-97, there were three cases of custodial rape, one each in Madhya Pradesh, Uttar Pradesh and Rajasthan. All cases of death in police or jail custody were not due to torture, but in some cases deaths due to torture came to light after investigation. In the year 1996-97[1], the NHRC asked its investigation division to probe into 23 cases of custodial death. In 14 of these cases, the police and jail staff concerned were held to be responsible for these deaths.

In its Annual Report (1995-96)[2] for prevention of custodial violence, the NHRC supported implementation of some of the recommendations made by the Indian Law Commission from time to time for prevention of violence and torture in police custody. In its 113th report in 1985, the Law Commission had suggested the insertion of section 114 (b) in the Indian Evidence Act, 1872, to introduce a rebuttable presumption that injuries sustained by a person in police custody may be presumed to have been caused by a police officer.

The NHRC also supported the recommendation of the Law Commission that section 197 of the Code of Criminal Procedure be amended to obviate the necessity of governmental sanction for the prosecution of a police officer where a Sessions Judge has established a prima facie case of a custodial offence against a police officer. The commission also endorsed the view of the National Police Commission that there should be a mandatory enquiry by a Sessions Judge in each case of custodial death, rape or grievous hurt.

While investigating into cases of torture in police and jail custody, the NHRC noticed with dismay the poor quality of post-mortem reports received by it. The commission felt that such reports may have been "doctored" under police or other extraneous pressures. The Chairman of NHRC wrote to the Chief Ministers on December 10, 1995 recommending that post-mortems of deaths in police or judicial custody should be video filmed and cassettes should be sent to the commission together with the written reports of the post-mortem examinations. The commission's recommendation have now been accepted by majority of the states. The commission has also transmitted to them a Model Autopsy Form and the Additional Procedure for Inquests after discussions with concerned officers in the states and experts around the country.

Role of the Supreme Court

The Supreme Court in India in a number of cases has taken a very firm stand against custodial violence and come forward to protect the rights of the victims. "Custodial violence is a calculated assault on human dignity 'And whenever the human dignity is wounded', as the Supreme Court observed in its judgement of December 18, 1996 in the case of 'D.K. Basu Vs The State of West Bengal[3], civilization takes a step backward. The flag of humanity on each occasion must fly half-mast".

In this landmark judgement the Supreme Court has laid down procedures to be followed in cases of arrest or detention till legal provisions are made as preventive measures. These requirements, inter alia, are:

- Police personnel carrying out arrests and handling the interrogation of an arrestee must wear accurate, visible and clear identification and name tags giving their designations. The particulars of all such personnel who handle interrogations must be recorded in a register:
- The police officer carrying out the arrest, must prepare memo of arrest at the time of arrest; this memo must be attested by a witness who may be either a member of the family of the arrestee or a responsible person of the locality from where the arrest has been made.

- The person arrested or detained shall be entitled to have a friend, a relative or other person known to him, or having an interest in his welfare informed, as soon as practicable.
- The arrestee should, when he so requests, be medically examined at the time of arrest and major injuries, if any are present on his or her body, must be recorded in memo. The inspection memo should be signed both by the arrestee and by the police officer concerned, and a copy should be given to the arrestee.
- The arrested person should undergo a medical examination by a trained doctor every forty-eight hours of his detention in custody.
- The arrestee should be permitted to meet his lawyer during interrogation.

The Supreme Court of India imparted a new dimension to the enforceability of these directions by attaching the sanction of contempt for breach or violation of these requirements. Failure to comply with the requirements will not only render the concerned officer liable for departmental action, he will also be liable to be punished for contempt of court.

In another path breaking judgement in the case of Francis Coralie Mullin[4] Vs the Union Territory of Delhi, the Supreme Court has interpreted that the state cannot deny any person the right to live with basic human dignity. Hence torture or degrading treatment which trenches on the human dignity would be impermissible under the Constitution. The Supreme Court has thus made immunity against torture or inhuman treatment as a fundamental right under Article 21of the Constitution. Article 7 of the International Covenant on Civil & Political Rights is thus woven into the constitutional jurisprudence of the country.

Causes

Now the question arises why police resort to torture and third degree methods which now and again lead to deaths in police custody. One of the causes of custodial deaths is the pressure on the police to detect cases whenever there is a surge in crime. There is relentless pressure on the police whenever there is an upswing in crime from the political masters as well as the public to resort to unethical means and render rough and ready justice not sanctioned by law against the anti-social elements who are escaping conviction and getting away scot-free because of the malfunctioning of the Criminal Justice System. The stark fact cannot be gainsaid that there is some amount of double-talking and double-thinking over the issue. Even the enlightened members of the society expect the police to take strong action not sanctioned by law against the anti-social elements. It is necessary for the senior Police Officers to resist such pressures and see that police function within the four-corners of law. Unfortunately, many officers fail to resist such pressures and give a free hand to the subordinates who tend to lose balance. As a result, not only the criminals but many innocent citizens become victims of police excesses. The struggle between the ends and means is thus a perpetual occupational dilemma for the police. This is known in police literature as the 'Dirty Harry' problem. The 'Dirty Harry' problem traces its name from the film 'Dirty Harry' and its chief protagonist and Inspector Harry. The heart of the problem involves juxtaposition of good ends and dirty means. It is important to remember that abuses of police can flourish not only because of official negligence or acquiescence but because, rightly or wrongly broad sections of the people under certain conditions and circumstances feel that the police in spite of their excesses are carrying out an unnecessary and unpleasant task for preserving and protecting the state and society. Custodial torture is thus a symptom of the malaise afflicting the police organisation.

In any analysis of the problems of torture in police custody, one has to keep in mind the difficult conditions in which the police function and the various types of hazards to which they are constantly exposed. Policemen are over stressed and over worked. The relaxation time is short and the problems of healthy recreation are non-existent. Recently a study conducted by Nimhans (National Institute of Mental Health & Sciences) of Bangalore on police personal of Delhi and certain districts of Karnataka has shown that the policemen live a life of high tension, suffer from poor health and often use intoxicants. There is also high prevalence of mental health problems among policemen. When a person is unable to enjoy his own rights fully, he is very often callous and disrespectful to those of the others.

The fact that should not be overlooked in this connection, is that the police violence and brutality are co-related to the public attitude towards the police. Lowered public regard reduces police self-esteem thereby making misuse of force by the police more likely. On the other hand, unwarranted and unbridled use of force goes to lower public esteem for the police. Thus, an element of circularity enters in the pattern Therefore, in countries like UK and Japan where police enjoy public confidence and regard, there are few occasions of brutal use of force by the police. But the situation is different in the USA. India and other developing countries, where public regard for the police is poor and instances of police brutality and violence are too frequent.

Compensation

In this connection, it is necessary to provide adequate compensation to the victims of police violence and torture. At present, there is no law governing the liability of the state for the wrong done to the citizens by a public servant in course of his employment. The only provision regarding payment of compensation is contained in Section 357 CRPC which provides for payment of compensation for a loss or injury caused by criminal offence to the victim after fine is imposed by the court. The provision does not make it mandatory for the state to pay compensation to the victims.

The courts in India, however, have granted compensation to the victims of custodial crimes or the family members in many cases. In the case of Rudul Sah[5] Vs State of Bihar, while awarding interim compensation for wrongful detention, the Supreme Court observed that "respect for rights of individuals is the bastion of democracy. Therefore, the state must repair the damage done by its officers to the petitioner's rights". However, the amount of compensation has not been uniform and cardinal principles have not been laid down. It is desirable to frame a suitable legislation under which the state should pay compensation to the victims of custodial crime or to their kith and kin. In a number of cases, the National Human Rights Commission has taken the view that the compensation due to the next of kin of those who have died in police custody should be liability not just of the state government but of the offending police officials themselves. This should provide a powerful deterrent to the aberrant behaviour of the lawless elements of the law enforcement profession.

To prevent custodial violence in police stations, it is necessary for senior officers of the police to make clear to the subordinates that use of torture against persons in custody will not be condoned and deterrent action will be taken against the perpetrators of such offences. It is also seen that though in a large number of cases of custodial deaths, officers responsible are suspended and departmental enquiries against them instituted, departmental enquiries drag on and ultimately very few offenders are brought to book. It is also a fact that many arrested persons in police or judicial custody in a state of acute mental depression commit suicide. It is necessary for senior officers visiting police stations or jails to see that no weapons or articles that can facilitate escape or suicide are within the reach of the arrestee in the lock up. Further, there should be constant exhortation by the senior officers to the subordinate staff at the cutting edge level that extra legal methods and torture are self-defeating and will expose them to legal and departmental action. During my long years of service in the police, I have seen that this kind of no-nonsense attitude and approach on the part of the senior officers will have a restraining impact on the members of the force down the line. It builds up an organisational climate that frowns upon abuse and misuse of authority and other forms of excesses.

Indeed, the roots of police deviance are deep-seated. Maurice Punch in a perceptive study 'Conduct Unbecoming'[6] has pointed out that police misconduct, as noticed in different countries of the world, results from 'ambiguous legislation, vulnerability to legal sanctions, occupational culture and pressure to produce quick results'. Hence the problem of 'Policing the Police' *(quis custodiet ipsos custodes)* has to be addressed seriously. For example, the power of arrest now available to the police is often misused to harass and humiliate persons in several situations prompted by malafide considerations. The National Police Commission in its report[7], after a study of police arrests in a few states, pointed out that by and large 60 per cent of these arrests were unnecessary and unjustified and such unorganised police action accounted for 43 per cent of the expenditure of the jails. Regarding making arrests by the police, the Supreme Court in the case of Joginder Kumar Vs State of Uttar Pradesh (1994 {3} SC 423) has laid down specific guidelines which must find place in all police manuals and regulations.

In this connection, it may be mentioned that the National Human Rights Commission in its submission before the Supreme Court in the matter of Prakash Singh and others Vs Union of India (Writ Petition No.310 of 1996) has while endorsing the recommendations of the National Police Commission for insulation of the investigation wing of the police from extraneous pulls and pressures and setting up of a Police Security Commission for laying down broad policy guidelines and directions for the performance of preventive tasks and service oriented functions of the police, has also suggested specific measures to make police 'high in accountability and low in authority'. It has suggested formation of District Police Complaints Authority to examine complaints from the public of police excesses and make appropriate recommendations to the government and National Human Rights Commission and State Human Rights Commissions wherever they have been set up. It has also recommended institution of 'Lay-Visitors' to jails and police lock-ups. The scheme will be similar to the one introduced in UK in the early 1980s on the recommendations of the Scarman Report. The visitors consisting of independent and respectable members of the public will visit police stations and police lock-ups to examine the conditions and report to the District Police Complaints Authority or to the State or National Human Rights Commission.

It is only through the working of both internal and external mechanisms of control, a human rights culture in the police can be built up. Sanction against errant officers for using violence inappropriately will not be adequate. Ceaseless vigilance and unremitting efforts on the part of the police leaders to build up a force which eschews unnecessary brutality and violence are called for. The basic principles on the use of Force and Firearms by Law-enforcement officials (adopted in September 1990 by the Eighth UN Congress on the prevention of Crime and Treatment of offenders) provide that "law enforcement agencies shall give special attention to the issue of police ethics and human rights, to alternatives to the use of force and fire-arm, including the peaceful settlement of conflicts, as well as technical means with a view to limiting the use of force and firearms".

REFERENCES

1. National Human Rights Commission, Annual Report 1996-97.
2. National Human Rights Commission, Annual Report 1995-96.
3. D.K. Basu Vs the State of West Bengal (Writ Petition CRL No. 539 of 1986).
4. Francis Coralie Mullin Vs Union Territory of Delhi (AIR 1981, SC 746).
5. AIR 1983, SC 1086.
6. 'Conduct Unbecoming'-Maurile Punch (pp. 2-3).
7. 'Corruption in Police'-Chapter XXII (pp. 30), Third Report of the National Police Commission.

Section—II

9
Police Autonomy and Accountability

The role of police in democratic societies is difficult and can unbelievably be thankless. The policeman's lot, to quote W.S. Gilbert, is not a happy one. From no other profession is so much demanded with so little recompense. Law vests police with the authority to use legitimate and situationally justified force against the citizens. This mandate to the police to use force to prevent violence raises the key issue that the police should not indulge in unnecessary violence or excessive use of force. With the fast and rapid growth of population and, urbanisation and the, collapse of societal values and norms, there is an upsurge in crime and violence.

The nature and face of crime is also changing. There is a surge in crime in the developed as well as developing countries and there are clear indications that crime will continue to rise all over the world and likely to get worse. Crime is committed by young males disproportionately between the age of 15 and 25 years. 29 per cent of serious crimes in the United States are committed by people under 19 years of age. This group will rise by over 20 per cent in the next decade. In Canada, 14 per cent of criminal violence and 25 per cent of crimes over property are committed by people between 15 and 17 years old. The lethality of crime is also sharply increasing everywhere. This is owing to the easy availability of illegal weapons, and firearms as also the spread of international terrorism, drug trafficking,[1] etc.

Police Professionalism

The police have to work in an everchanging society, and to quote the Royal Commission on the Police (1962), "There is nothing constant about the range and variety of police duties just as there is nothing constant about the pattern of crime and hidden trends in society that dispose man to crime." Policing today has become complex and requires a high degree of professionalism. Increased professionalisation should be the hallmark of policing in the coming days. A professional is a person who has developed himself thoroughly in the concerned field and has enriched himself in experience and self-confidence on which proper performance of duties depends. The old concept of the police officer as 'a Renaissance Man' who, once he affixes the badge, becomes magically able to perform any job regardless of interest and personality style, must be done away with. With professionalism the police have also to develop a proper code of conduct to win the confidence and respect of the citizens.

Further, the police agencies have some peculiar characteristics which call for professional management. Police officers are often spread out in the field and are not subject to direct supervision. Officers also enjoy awesome authority and discretion in matters relating to the life and liberty of citizens. Difficult and unforeseen situations arise in police work and an error in judgement at a critical juncture may have disastrous consequences. Failure to properly manage an organisation with these characteristics results in exceptionally high costs. Very often police succumb to favouritism and political influence. Along with greater operating efficiency, fast responses, efficient use of time, smooth flow of paper work, the police should also act within the four corners of law and respect the constitutional rights of the citizens. The paramilitary heritage of the police has to be given up to make way for a more professional, humanistic and service-oriented police administration.

For proper functioning as an expert professional body, it is absolutely essential that the police which is vested with vast coercive power, should be able to function according to the rules of law and not on the whims or dictates of others. In a democratic society, there should be not interference from any quarter in the discharge of the lawful duties by the police. Totalitarian States are called 'Police States' because not only does the police enjoy unlimited and unbridled authority but very remains totally vulnerable to extra-legal pressures and influence.

Constabulary Independence

In Great Britain, the Royal Commission of Police in its Final Report (1962), while discussing the constitutional status of the police stated as follows: "The case of *Fisher vs. Oldham Corporation* established that whatever else he might be, the constable was not a servant of any organ of the local government. This view was approved by the Judicial Committee of the Privy Council in the case of *Attorney General for New South Wales vs. Perpetual Trustee Company.* The constitutional position of a constable is described as that of an officer whose authority is original and not delegated and is exercised at his discretion by virtue of his office. He is a ministerial officer exercising statutory rights independent of control."

Lord Denning, the former Master of the Rolls, commenting in the famous case of *R.vs. Metropolitan Police Commissioner Exp. Blackburn, 1968,* further entrenched chief officers' independent nature by stating that they were answerable to the "law and law alone." In the same case Lord Justice Salmon stated that, "Constitutionally it is clearly impermissible for the Home Secretary to issue any orders to the police in respect of law enforcement." More recently, in *R. vs. Oxford Exp. Levey, 1986,* Master of the Rolls Sir John Donaldson stated that, "the chief constables have the widest possible discretion".[2]

The doctrine of constabulary independence does give police officers in Great Britain a legitimate measure of discretion, but the British Police also remain exceptionally accountable, despite their independence of government institutions. Sir Robert Mark, a distinguished Commissioner of London Metropolitan Police, observed: "The fact that the British Police is answerable to law, and that it acts on behalf of the community and not under the mantle of the government, makes them the least powerful, the most accountable and the most acceptable police in the world".[3]

In this connection, perhaps it will be useful to examine the internal autonomy of the police as prevalent in some other democratic countries. In Japan, there is National Public Safety Commission (NPSC), an apex body which comprises the Chairman with Ministers of State and five other members appointed with the consent of both the Houses of the Diet. At the local level, police affairs are dealt with by the prefectural police force. There is the Prefectural Public Safety Commission (PPSC) consisting of three to five members according to the size of the prefecture. Both the NPSC and PPSC are insulated from political pressures and neither the Prime Minister nor the Prefectural Governor have the power to give them any directions whatsoever.

In India, as far back as 1902-03, the Frazer Commission, 'while reviewing the working of the police, acidly commented that a number of rules and regulations framed by the Provincial Governments were contrary to the spirit of the Police Act of 1861 and there had been a degree of interference which the law did not contemplate and which had been prejudicial to the interests of the police department. After the dawn of independence it was hoped that the degree of interference in the working of the police will diminish and police officers will be allowed to function as neutral custodians of law and order without external pulls and pressures. Unfortunately, that did not happen and constant interference in police work over time has made police ineffective and totally eroded its autonomy.

Politicians leaders have unabashedly used their powers of arbitrary posting, transfer, punishment, promotion to bully and browbeat officers into submission. Unfortunately, section 3 of the Police Act, 1861 provides that superintendence of the "police throughout the general police district" shall vest in and shall be exercised by the State Government to which the district is subordinate. This provision of the Act has been utilised by the State authorities to unabashedly interfere in the proper working of the police. In the words of a perceptive American writer, Prof. David H. Bayley in 'Police and Political Development in India', "altogether rule of law in modern India, the frame upon which justice hangs, has been undermined by the rule of politics. Supervision in the name of democracy has eroded the foundations upon which impartiality depends in the criminal justice system."

Recently, the former Home Minister, Mr Indrajit Gupta, in a letter to all the Chief Ministers, (on April 3, 1997) said that "the popular perception all over the country appears to be that many of the deficiencies in the functioning of the police in our country have arisen largely due to overdose of unhealthy and petty political interference at various levels starting from transfer and posting of policemen of different ranks, misuse of police for partisan purposes and political patronage quite often extended to corrupt police personnel. In fact, within the police forces also there is strong resentment against political and other extraneous interference in the discharge of their lawful and professional duties."

Prof. David H. Bayley4 has perceptively written that "India which should have been expected to transform the organisation of police rapidly after independence, has exactly kept the same system which the British created in 1861. The control mechanism of British Raj has survived and been invigorated by a new political dispensation." He further adds that it is interesting to note that during the last decade "the Chief Minister of every State has taken over the direction of the Ministry of Home Affairs." This is a dramatic indication of the importance of the police in political life in contemporary India. Contrast this with the relative position of the Home Secretary and Chancellor of Exchequer in Britain or comparable positions in Canada and the United States where money is much more important than law enforcement in politics.[5]

While dealing with the issue of police autonomy, the National Police Commission made a number of important recommendations. The National Police Commission[6], inter-alia, recommended that:

(a) It is necessary to insulate the investigation wing of the police from external pressures to ensure its freedom in the operational areas of police investigation.

(b) To remove the proverbial Damocles' Sword of transfer dangling constantly on the head of the chief of the police and assuring him a statutory tenure after proper and careful selection.

(c) Constitution of State Security Commission to help the State Government to effectively discharge its superintending responsibility under the framework of law.

Views of the National Human Rights Commission

The National Human Rights Commission of India also endorsed7 these three critical and important recommendations of the National Police Commission in the interest of 'improving the human rights situation in the country'. It felt that there is a yearning in the nation for an "upright police force functioning with propriety and fairness which can be relied upon to protect the rights of the citizens of India".

Further, the Commission has impleaded itself as a party in the Supreme Court case of *Prakash Singh and other vs. Union of India.* In its counter-affidavit not only has the Commission referred to the doctrine of constabulary independence as in the UK, but also dealt with the practice prevailing in some other countries like Canada, New Zealand, etc. In Canada, the police forces at all levels are independent operationally and only respond to operative directives emanating from within the force. In terms of Federal Police Functions, the Royal Canadian Mounted Police (RCMP) reports to the Federal Solicitor General, broadly equivalent to the Home Minister in India. At provincial level the police force, reports to the Provincial Solicitor General but there is no interference at any level in the operational activities of the police. In New Zealand, the Police Act of 1988, ensures that the police are not subject to the directions given by the Minister in-charge in matters of law-enforcement. The constitutional relationship between the Police Commissioner and the Minister of Police differs from that of the chief executives of all other government agencies and their ministers. While responsible to the Minister of Police for general administration of the police, the Commissioner is not subject to the directions of the ministers in matters of operational law enforcement in particular cases. The Commissioner remains independent of the government in terms of his duties to direct law-enforcement strategies.

The National Human Rights Commission, however, felt strongly that police autonomy should be balanced by police accountability. The police in a democratic society "must be low in authority and high in accountability. The police must be accountable to law and function with in the four corners of law. To ensure that police autonomy does not result in the creation of a Frankenstein-like monster, appropriate checks and controls are needed. For this purpose, the Commission suggested mandatory judicial inquiry into all cases of custodial death and rape, setting up of District Complaints Authority to examine grievances of the public in matters of misuse of power, wrongful arrests and custodial violence by the police and making appropriate recommendations to the State Government or to National Human Rights Commission for necessary action, as also introduction of 'Lay Visitors Scheme' for visiting police lockups similar to the one introduced in the UK in the early 1980s on the recommendations of the Scarman Report. For a group of police stations in every district, the government, in consultation with State Human Rights Commission or the National Human Rights Commission as the case may be, will form a group of responsible members of the public to visit police stations and lockups to examine the conditions and report to the District Complaints Authority. The Lay Visitors shall not be entitled to interfere in any manner in the functioning of the police and report its findings only to District Complaints Authority or to the respective State Human Rights Commissions.

Accountability: Meaning and Dimensions

Accountability, as the National Police Commission mentioned in its Eighth Report, means answerability for the proper performance of the assigned task. While it is true that the ultimate accountability of the police is to the people, the police have the proximate accountability to the law of the land which is the expression of popular will. As a law-enforcing agency, the activities of the police centre around the enforcement of laws; the functioning of the police is also governed by the processes of laws. It is aptly said that the relationship of the police to law is instrumental as well as professional. It is a tool in their hands for initiating action against the offending members of the public, while it also lays down the standards under which the police will execute their duties. Indeed, an independent and abusive police, presents a fundamental problem for the legitimacy of the legal and political order. Exercise of power by the police must be subject to checks and balances. The system of checks and balances, if they are to serve the intended purposes, must be reliable as well as effective in their operation.

Again, regulation of police misconduct can be internal as well as external. Prof. Bayley has argued in his book Pattern of Policing—A Comparative International Analysis that internal control has to be preferred to external processes as regulation can be more effective. A determined police can indeed hide many things from external supervision and make it haphazard and confusing. Further, internal regulation can be more thorough and extensive and can focus upon the entire gamut of police operations and not mere dramatic aberrations. However, experience in different countries of the world has shown that exclusive reliance upon police self-regulation is not sufficient. External regulation is necessary wherever it is felt that police force on its own cannot control itself. This is the reason why civilian oversight of the police has emerged as one of the legitimate means to exercise check on the abuse of police power.

However, there is another aspect of the issue which has to be carefully kept in mind. Civilian oversight can also open proper channels of communication between the police and citizenry. In a democracy there is remote control over the conduct of the police by the representatives of the people. Civilian oversight offers a direct proximate opportunity for criticism and control of police conduct. Normally, relationship between the police and the community is not based upon proper understanding of each other's needs and problems. Civilian oversight will go a long way to restore a two-way dialogue based upon concern and respect and replace the taciturn, and at times hostile, relationship between the police and the community. Further, civilian oversight no doubt makes police organisation more open and transparent. Historically, police organisations in many countries of the world have adopted hierarchical, military organisational structure which does not welcome criticisms either from the subordinates or outsiders. Open policing will encourage proper and healthy criticisms from outsiders as well as members of the organisation.

Lord Scarman in his report after the Brixton disorder (10-12th April, 1981) mentioned that, "The police must exercise independent judgement, but they are also servants of the community. They enforce law on behalf of the community. Indeed, they cannot effectively enforce it without the support of the community. The community pays them and provides resources. So there has to be some way to secure that the independent judgement of the police cannot only operate within the law, but also with the support of the community." In1967 in the USA, the task force on the police of the 'President's Commission on Law Enforcement and Administration of Justice'9 declared: "without question the best means for ensuring that the police personnel comply with the departmental policy is through effective internal procedures. Internal discipline can be swifter because it is imposed on officers by the superiors and is more effective than external review." US Commission for Civil Rights, 1967, however, expressed a different view. It quotes the observation of the former US Attorney General, Ramsay Clark, that Police Review Boards in which citizens' panels finally determine the allegations of police misconduct and appropriate penalties are desirable. "Some civilian review of police conduct, whatever be the form, is always essential. Ultimately, the police are responsible to the public and not to the chief of the police."

In 1991, an audit was made on five years of complaints processed by the Los Angeles Police Department. The review revealed that a large number of complaints have been written off without proper inquiry or any justifiable reason. The Christopher Commission which looked into the working of Los Angeles Police Department after the Rodney King incident said that sometimes the citizens have to wait for hours in the police stations if they have had to lodge a complaint against the police. It could be seen that the police will very often suppress complaints of abuse of authority treating them as minor in nature with a view to avoiding review process altogether. Thus, a large number of complaints could be quashed at the initial intake level.

The police professionals and administrators frown upon the civilian review often as an intrusion into their profession and feel that they themselves understand the difficulties of the profession much better than those who are not a part of it. There is also internal solidarity and a desire not to blow the whistle on a colleague.

However, mechanisms within the police organisation to control itself vary from country to country. In Japan, the police authorities themselves are virtually sovereign in respect of internal control. Though there are Public Safety Commissions to oversee overall management of the force, the police authorities are supreme in respect of internal control. In Canada also, disciplinary decisions within the Royal Canadian Mounted Police are not subject to court review. The Commissioner may award up to 30 days of imprisonment to erring officers without trial. The problem in India is that the command and control of the senior officers have been significantly eroded by political interference and also at times by the courts. Authority has been transferred to political bosses and the courts. In this connection, it may be mentioned that internal control is strengthened if formal command procedures are supplemented by some kind of willingness of personnel to discipline one another with firmness. "Japanese police officers", David H. Bayley10 reports, "almost always work in pairs with the understanding that one officer is responsible to ensure the propriety of the other's behaviour. American officers on the other hand mostly work alone and even while working together, they are reluctant to be critical of one another. In India too, constables work in groups, but they do not seem to control or restrain one another. Internal control is affected significantly by the organisational culture. A study11 by the Vera Institute of Justice, New York on investigation of police misconduct led to the conclusion that "making the Review Board independent of the department and drafting more civilian investigators won't change the outcome of most investigations. Experience of civilian review in some of the American cities suggest that civilian review is less likely than police internal review to find officers guilty of misconduct and is more lenient in its disciplinary recommendations when it finds them guilty".

The experience in India, however, is different. While working in the National Human Rights Commission, the present writer has observed that the Commission's investigators exposed many cases of abuse and misuse of authority by the police which the police authorities were trying to shove under the carpet. After investigation by the officers of NHRC, the police authorities in many cases had to start investigation, afresh and take action against the delinquent officials. If the matter was left for internal control, the lapses would never have come to light. In the NHRC more than 60 per cent of the complaints are against the abuse of power and misuse of authority by the police. The fact that has to be borne in mind is that the number of complaints received is not necessarily related to prevalence and extent of police abuse. It may often be related to the public confidence in the review process and the manner in which the complaints are handled. It is true that many complaints are without merit. It is also difficult to authenticate many complaints because of lack of evidence, but it many cases, gross abuse of authority by the police have been proved to the hilt.

In any inquiry into allegations of police misconduct, it is essential that parties to the complaint—both citizens and the police, should be given an opportunity to present to the decision-making authority all the information they deem relevant. They should also express their perceptions of the matter at issue. The victims of police misconduct should be treated with due care and concern. Procedural fairness effect is also produced by parties' perception whether the decision-maker is fair and impartial. Hence, the decision-making authority must command credibility and respect. To create a perception of fairness, both parties must feel that their point of view has been given due weightage and consideration. A credible decision-maker can make unfavourable outcome more convincing. Procedural justice research has shown that judgements about fairness, both procedural and distributive, are key determinants of the citizens' attitude towards decision-makers, the decision-making process, institutions and the social structure itself.

From the mass of complaints against the police useful conclusions can sometimes be drawn. In Los Angeles, the Christopher Commission and court investigations made the discovery that a relatively small number of officers accounted for a large number of complaints. Many other useful conclusions can be reached if the complaints are tracked and analysed in a systematic manner.

International human rights standards also firmly emphasise police accountability. International human rights standards concerning torture, misuse of authority, excessive use of force are spelt out in the Universal Declaration of Human Rights, International Covenants on Civil and Political Rights, Convention on Torture, Code of Conduct for Law Enforcement Officers and the Basic Principles on Use of Force and Fire Arms by the police officials. They condemn abuse of authority or excessive or unnecessary use of force by the police. In India, the code for law-enforcement officials has been incorporated in the Code of Conduct for Police Officials issued by the Ministry of Home Affairs. In many countries of the developing world, Human Rights Commissions have been created owing to profects about violation of international standards. International standards increase the cutting edge because they seek to establish systems of review and oversight for abuse by force. Article 22 of the Basic Principles in Use of Force and Fire Arms directs that: "Government and law enforcement agencies shall ensure that effective review process is available and it is independent of administrative or prosecutoral authority and the concerned authorities are in a position to exercise jurisdiction in appropriate circumstances." Similarly, the Convention against Torture requires that law enforcement officers should be trained in proper methods of interrogation.

Article 2 of the United Nations Code of Conduct for Law-enforcement Officials mentions that in the performance of duty, law enforcement officials shall respect and protect human dignity and uphold the human rights of all persons. Demands for some mode of civilian oversight in countries facing international criticisms over the conduct of police forces is fast emerging. In the case of Brazil, the United Nations Human Rights Committee in its Fifty-seventh Session considering the Brazil's Report, submitted under Article 40 of the International Covenants on Civil and Political Rights recommended in paragraph 22 that "all complaints of misconduct by members of security force be investigated by an independent body and not by the security forces. Further, such mechanism must make provision for effective protection for the complainants and witnesses against intimidation and reprisals."

The National Police Commission has also highlighted another peculiar problem faced by the police in India. It is seen that on occasions false and frivolous complaints with a view to embarrassing and demoralising officers are made so that they desist from taking action against the offending parties. The law has provided protection to police officers as well as government servants for acts done or purported to be done in the discharge of their official duties. Section 197 of the Code of Criminal Procedure provides protection to judges, magistrates and all public servants and are not removable from their office except by or with the sanction of the government.

The National Police Commission recommended that the public should be free to seek the verdict of the court of law it has grievance against a government servant. The National Police Commission, however, did not endorse the suggestion making it obligatory for the public complainant to deposit a certain amount of money along with the complaint in a court of law. The amount will be subjected to forfeiture if the complaint is found to be false. The Commission felt that such a provision will prevent the weaker sections of the society from going to the courts of law to seek redressal of their grievances. The Commission has recommended, nevertheless, that if the complaint is unfounded, there should be legal provision to inflict suitable punishment on the complainant. The Law Reforms Commission appointed by the Australian Government in its report on "Complaints against the Police" recommended that where the complaints filed against a police officer concerning the action taken by him is found to be false or misleading in material particulars, it should be treated as an offence punishable with a fine of $ 500 and imprisonment up to six months. The Commission recommended introduction of a similar legal provision.

For ensuring accountability, people should be made aware of their rights and they should be willing to exercise the same in a responsible manner. Public awareness should also include the realisation of difficulties and constraints under which the police function. The police should on their part understand, to quote the observations of the National Police Commission that "their ultimate accountability is to the people and people alone. Their accountability to the law and to the organisation are only complementary to the ultimate objective of accountability to the people."

REFERENCES

1. David H. Bayley and Christopher D. Shearing "Future of Policing", Law and Society Review, Vol. 30, No. 3, 1996.
2. Practical Police Management, p. 20, by Geoff Berry Jim Izat Rob Mawby Lynne Walley.
3. Sir Robert Mark: "Policing a Perplexed Society".
4. David H. Bayley: "Patterns of Policing—A Comparative International Analysis".
5. *Ibid.*, p.164.
6. Second Report of the National Police Commission, Chapter XV, 1979.
7. National Human Rights Commission, Annual Report, 1995-96.
8. Eighth Report of the National Police Commission, pp.1-11.
9. *Understanding and Controlling Police Abuse of Force,* p. 206.
10. David H. Bayley, "Patterns of Policing—A Comparative International Analysis", p. 168.
11. *New York Times,* October 23, 1992 quoted by Wayne A. Kerstretter in the article 'Procedural Justice Perspective on Police and Citizen Satisfaction with Investigations of Police Use of Force—Finding a Common Ground of Fairness'.

10
Policing the Police-Experience in the United Kingdom

In modern democratic societies, the police are vested with the authority of using legitimate and situationally justified force against the citizens. The police may use force to protect rights of the citizens and it may also use it in a manner that imperils citizen's rights and liberties. Arbitrary and unchecked use of power by the police spells threats to a civil society. Hence, exercise of police powers must be subject to effective checks and balances. Heie, important point to remember is that these checks and balances should be perceived as effective and dependable by members of the public. Experience of dealing with police misconduct in different parts of the world shows that exclusive reliance on police self-regulation is not always sufficient. Capacity of the police to regulate itself is limited and does not carry conviction with the people. This is the reason why civilian oversight of the police has emerged as one of the legitimate means by the State authorities to exercise checks on police powers.

The functioning of the Police Complaints Authority in United Kingdom, in this connection, provides many useful lessons and warnings. In the United Kingdom, the Police and Criminal Evidence Act, 1984, set up the Police Complaints Authority to replace the Police Complaints Board.

In April 1981, UK witnessed Brixton disorders when in the centre of Brixton, hundreds of young people, not all of them black, attacked the police on the streets with stones, bricks and iron bars and petrol and demonstrated to the millions of their fellow-citizens the 'fragile basis of the Queen's Peace'.

Lord Scarman who enquired into the Brixton disorders, mentioned in his report about 'a widespread and dangerous lack of public confidence in the existing system for handling complaints against the police'. In his report, Scarman made a number of recommendations to improve the quality of police service in the United Kingdom. He wrote that "the law must be sensitively as well as firmly applied. If the police neglect consultation and cooperation of the local community, unrest is certain and riot becomes probable". One of his important recommendations was constitution of Police Complaints Authority.

The Police Complaints Authority set up under the Police and Criminal Evidence Act (PCEA) replaced the Police Complaints Board (PCB). Independent Police Complaints Board was established by the Police Act of 1976. Establishment of the PCB evoked strong protests from the police. Sir Robert Mark, the well-known Commissioner of London Metropolitan Police, resigned over the setting up of the PCB. The PCB, however, failed to command public confidence because of its lack of independent investigative powers and pro-establishment character of its members. It was totally reliant on investigation done by the police and seldom over-ruled the internal police decision not to bring charges in most of the cases. The new Police Complaints Authority (PCA) which replaced the PCB has the powers to recommend, and if necessary, direct bringing of disciplinary charges against the police officers on receipt of complaints from the members of the public. It also acquired powers to supervise directly, complaints alleging serious injury or death caused by police abuse. It is also empowered to do so in other cases when it considers necessary in public interest.

The PCA is organized into two divisions—one consisting of a deputy chairman and five members to carry out supervisory functions. The other composed of a deputy chairman and six members performing the job of review and adjudication. The Act provides that the complaints must be made by or on behalf of a member of the public about the conduct of a serving officer and may not relate to the direction and control of the force. Every year about 1600 people contact the PCA with various forms of complaints against the police. The legislation provides for informal resolution of the less serious complaints. About 40 per cent of the complaints are dealt in this way without reaching the Authority. However, if the complainant is dissatisfied with the outcome of informal resolution, he is entitled to press for settlement of his complaint through the formal processes.

The Police and Criminal Evidence Act, 1984 defines the types of cases which must be referred to the Authority for supervision. The Authority must supervise all complaints relating of death or serious injury caused by police abuse. In respect of other cases, it is for PCA to decide whether it will supervise or not. Section 88 of the Act also provides that police forces can ask the Authority to supervise any case not based on complaint but commission of an offence by an officer, like deaths in police custody or acts of serious corruption or misconduct.

The PCA has no separate investigating agency. It relies upon police investigators. It selects police officers from different police forces and lays down the requirements for proper conduct of the investigation. On completion of the investigation, a report is submitted to the Chief of the Force concerned and the latter is to decide on the basis of the report if the officer has committed a criminal offence and if he should be charged. If a view is taken to charge to the officer, the case is referred to the Crown Prosecution Service (CPS) to decide whether or not to prosecute the officer. The Authority has the power to direct that the case be referred to CPS, even though the Chief of the Force has decided not to do so. The regulations also permit the Authority to grant dispensation from the need to investigate a complaint if it is anonymous or repetitive, vexatious or involves abuse of procedures or if there is more than one year delay between the incident and the complaint or if it is not reasonably practical to carry out an investigation. As granting of exemption really means that a citizen's statutory right to have his complaint investigated is removed, the applications for dispensation are carefully scrutinized and the complainants are made aware of the reasons before granting dispensation.

The Report "Police Complaints Authority—The First Ten Years" refers to some of the major investigations supervised by the PCA. In 1991, PCA enquired into the allegations against the West Midlands Police's Serious Crime Squad. The Authority's review resulted in seven officers facing disciplinary charges of falsehood and prevarication and a further 102 were advised about their failure to follow force procedures. The Authority also submitted a special report to the Home Secretary on the working practices of the Serious Crime Squad. There were detailed recommendations regarding safeguarding of evidence, supervision of payments to the informants and working on overtime. The report was published by the Home Office and the Chief Constable took prompt steps to implement the recommendations. The supervised enquiry into complaint against the West Midlands Serious Crime Squad led directly or indirectly to the convictions of 22 men being quashed.

In 1994, the PCA carried out a major investigation into allegations against 45 officers based at Stroke Newington Police Station in East London. The investigation known as 'Operation Jackpot' covered 24 cases and involved 134 allegations against police officers ranging from assault, conspiracy to pervert the cause of justice, planting of drugs, etc.

After considering the final report, the Crown Prosecution Service decided to prosecute two officers on the charges of perjury and conspiracy to pervert the course of justice.

Article 98 of the Police and Criminal Evidence Act makes it a criminal offence for any member or officer of the Police Complaints Authority to publish or disclose an information arising out of investigation. It does permit publication of a summary, but this must not identify the person from whom the information was received or any person to whom it relates. The PCA has felt that while there is need to protect the complainants and the witnesses, it should have the discretion to disclose as much details as it believes is necessary in public interest. It maintains that Section 98 of the Act is a major obstacle in the building of public confidence.

A major study evaluating the PCA was done by Maguire and Corbett in 1991 (Complaints against the police—The trend to External Review—Edited by Andrew J. Goldsmith). It revealed that the system has failed to command adequate confidence from the complainants, the police and members of the public. In majority of the cases, allegations of misconduct against the police remain unsubstantiated. Earlier with the Police Complaints Board during the period from 1979-89, out of a total of 330109 complaints, 13790, only 4 per cent of the complaints, could be substantiated. The advent of PCA did not bring about any substantial difference in the overall result. In 1989, there were only 765 substantiations out of the 9229 complaints fully investigated. The study further says that many of the junior police officers have adopted a "cavalier" and "don't care" attitude to the complaints. Only a small percentage of officers felt that they feel demoralised as the complaints put them in a negative light. Not only many complainants felt that the PCA was on the side of the police, even some of the police officers including a Metropolitan Police Commissioner did acknowledge that the public does not have much faith in the PCA.

The PCA in its turn tried to gauge the public feelings and perceptions through annual surveys of public attitudes towards the complaints system in general and the Authority in particular. The surveys show that the Authority still faces an uphill task to win public confidence and this lack of confidence is more evident among the minority ethnic communities. In his foreword to the publication 'Police Complaints Authority—The First Ten Years', Lord Scarman has written "For ten years the Police Complaints Authority has suffered the verbal slings and arrows of outraged politicians and the media. It would be seen that many had expected the Authority to correct all wrongs and weaknesses they believed to exist in our system of policing and it had not done so". The PCA in its various reports has emphasised the point that even the most minor disciplinary charges against a police officer must be proved "beyond reasonable doubt or dismissed". This very high standard of proof raises problems when there is a conflict of evidence between a police officer and the complainant with no corroboration on either side. By contrast, for civil action the standard of proof is based on the "balance of probabilities". As a result, it is often possible that a complaint may not result in any disciplinary action against the officers involved, but the complainant will be subsequently successful in any civil action against the officer. Since 1991, the PCA is pressing for a more flexible approach and with regard to the standard of proof based on "balance of probabilities". It hopes that this change should be introduced in the new police discipline system. Normally, complainants informed after many months that the complaints could not be substantiated, feel discouraged and dissatisfied. Mike Maguire's study shows that some of the complainants were making the first complaints against the police in their lives and felt that it is like "walking up to a six-feet man". They expect some form of redress or at least an apology or assurance that steps would be taken to prevent a recurrence.

There is now demand for full-blown investigation by an outside agency. However, there is also a feeling that if outsiders investigate all complaints, the resource implications would be substantial and one might be replacing "one unwieldy bureaucratic system with another". Some progressive Commissioners like Sir Peter Imbert (Imbert P. Glasnost at the Scotland Yard—Police Review, December,1989) felt that the standard of the burden of proof might have to be changed and the maintenance of the right of silence in the face of disciplinary investigation has to be reconsidered. But the fact has to be kept in mind that proper handling of complaints against the police is just one piece of the jig-saw, without improvement in training, police-public consultation, stricter supervision, it will not be possible for the police to gain public confidence. Improved methods of handling complaints against the police is only one important step in that direction.

11
Trends in American Policing

During the last thirty years a number of significant changes have occurred in American policing. The appointment of the President's Commission on Law Enforcement and Administration of Justice (1966) indeed marks the beginning of the period of great changes in American policing. The Commission's report "The Challenge of Crime in a Free Society" analysed the criminal justice system, diagnosed its failures and prescribed far-reaching changes and improvements. It also questioned the ability of the police to address the complex social issues that were the root causes of crime. A few years later, the Commission on Civil Disorder (Kerner Commission) and the Commission on the Causes and Prevention of Violence (the Eisenhower Commission) added significant observations on the problem of crime and the need for effective policing. The Kerner Commission, entrusted with the mission of analysing the civil disorder that rocked America during the decade, found that actual or rumoured excesses by the police were the major factors behind many of the disturbances that had erupted during the period.

In this connection it may be mentioned that at the beginning of the 1960s many police departments in America were totally closed to outside. Their personnel were drawn from particular groups related to one another by blood or ethnic origin. Little public debate took place over police procedures and practices and the police departments were seldom engaged in any experimentation and innovation.

The 1960s also saw galloping rise in crime in the USA. Crimes rose eight times more rapidly than the population growth, and the reported crimes accounted for only one-third of the number of crimes actually committed. The crime scene in the USA is now different. Serious crimes have declined for the nation as a whole. The National Crime Victimisation Survey, Crime Trends Data (1973-96) published by the Bureau of Justice Statistics indicate that rapes declined by 60 per cent from 1991 to 1996, robberies by 17 per cent and aggravated assaults by 27 per cent. The victimisation data show that total violent crime went down 19 per cent from 1994 to 1996. Property crimes are also on the decline for the nation as a whole according to the National Crime Victimisation Survey. Academics, criminologists and law enforcement officials have suggested many factors like increase in incarceration rates, policy shifts producing longer prison terms, low unemployment rates due to America's economic prosperity, increased public intolerance for crimes and various forms of disorderly conduct are responsible for the declining crime trend. Widespread innovations in police practices have also made a major contribution for this happy trend—from zero tolerance campaign in the New York City to community policing strategies involving problem-solving elsewhere.

The 1998 New York City Mayor's Management Report indicates that during the period from 1993 to 1997, the number of felony complaints dropped in New York City by 44 per cent. This includes a 60.2 per cent drop in murders, 12 per cent drop in rape, 48 per cent drop in robbery and 45.7 per cent drop in burglary. The New York City Mayor Rudy Guiliani and officers of the New York Police Department feel proud for bringing about this transformation in the crime situation in the city.. Howard Safir, the Police Commissioner of New York claims that New York has now become 'the safest largest city in the country'. (Report of the New York City Police Foundation, 1996).

One of the important crime control strategies in New York is introduction of the Compstat System (it was introduced by the Police Commissioner William Bratton) which puts up-to-date crimes data in the hands of the police managers at all levels and ensures precinct level accountability for crime reduction. In the biweekly Compstat Sessions (I attended such a session recently as the guest of the New York Police Commissioner) coordinated strategies are worked out for crime control and the Precinct Commanders have to explain the steps they have taken or propose to take to deal with the crimes that have occurred.

Improvements in American Police

It can be said generally that intellectual and professional standards of the American police have improved dramatically. The American police today of all ranks are better informed and more sophisticated and professionally more competent than the police in 1960s. There has been stress on professional model of policing which sought to achieve a higher level of operating efficiency by emphasising standard operating procedures fast responses, efficient use of time, and clean modern facilities. Further, the American police force today is more diverse in terms of race, colour and gender than it was 30 years ago. Today, there is increasing presence of the ethnic minorities in the different police forces in the USA. The number of female officers is also fast rising. The American police is thus changing in appearance, and more slowly, in its behaviour.

There has been significant application of policing research to real problems faced by the police who serve the troubled communities. Research findings on policing have challenged many existing practices and beliefs. A research study on Kansas City Preventive Patrol Experiment undertaken by the Police Foundation of Washington found that randomised patrolling had a very limited impact on crime or in citizen's attitude and in most cases rapid response by the police did not help to solve the crime. It was found that in respect of a large number of cases, the time taken by the public to report the crime to the police was the primary determinant of the eventual outcome. This research finding shifted the emphasis away from the response time and led the way for managing calls for service (an important tool for community policing).

The San Diego Police Department conducted several significant research studies which included a community-oriented policing (COP) project which was the first empirical study of community policing. The project demonstrated that developing stronger ties with the members of the communities was more important than that once believed and interaction with the community could improve the attitude of the officers towards their jobs and towards the communities they served and could encourage them to develop creative solutions to complex problems.

Many findings from this study have a direct bearing on contemporary community policing efforts. In 1979, Herman Goldstein developed the concept of problem-oriented policing (POP) which have encouraged the police to think differently about their purpose. Goldstein suggested that problem resolution constituted the true work of policing and advocated that the police should identify and address the root causes of problems that plagued the police. It called for a shift away from reactive incident-driven stance to one that deals with the real causes of the problems constantly requiring police attention.

The standards of police conduct have also improved. Experts like Prof. David. H. Bayley are of the view that despite some well-publicised cases of brutality and corruption, the American police today treat the public "more fairly, more equitably and less venally than police did thirty years ago" (David H. Bayley: Policing in America—Assessment and Prospects).

Civilian review of police work and conduct is also gaining wider acceptance by the police. At one time, the American police used to look askance at the civilian oversight bodies, but nowadays many police chiefs are veering round to the view that civilian review goes to reinforce and not weaken public confidence in the police and enables the police to forge closer links with the community.

Many police administrators, though not always enthusiastic about civilian review are not antagonistic to it. They feel that there is no inconsistency between civilian review and impartial and effective police administration. Samuel Walker's recent study shows that by 1992, 33 of the 50 largest cities of America had adopted civilian review of policing in some form. This development has already taken place in Canada, Australia, Great Britain, Denmark, and other Western countries and now it seems that corner has been turned in the USA too. There are also a few significant developments which are going to profoundly affect the future of American policing. In the USA today, there are as many private policemen as public. Important territorial areas like business premises and hotels are exclusively policed by private agents. There is now a growing dualism in policing in all developed nations with public police providing security for the poor and private police providing security for the rich.

Civilianisation

Another important development is the civilianisation of the police forces in different states. Civilianisation has become attractive because sworn police officers have become very costly. Captains of the police forces in places like Santa Anna and Oakland earn more than Professors at the University of California at Berkley or Los Angeles. Civilians are performing many clerical and communication tasks necessary to policing. Civilians are also inducted to other support areas such as research and training, forensic analysis, equipment maintenance. In some places civilians wearing police uniforms almost identical to sworn officers investigate traffic accidents, take crime reports, mediate neighbourhood disputes, etc. This arrangements is cost-effective and allows police to concentrate on its core functions. It also builds closer links between the police and the community. In the coming years, there will be more professional civilian support for the police service in the USA. Sworn police officers, however, fear that cost-saving civilianisation efforts will eventually bring about salary reduction and affect their prospects.

However, in many places in the USA, organised crime and group violence pose serious problems. Crime in America has become more violent because of the lethality of the weapons now available with the criminals. Technology has raised the potential destructiveness of criminal actions. If group violence and terrorism become more widespread, it will go to encourage a warfare mindset in the police. Many criminologists fear that community policing strategies with problem-solving orientation will then suffer a setback. Policing will then become more enforcement-oriented rather than ameliorative.

12
Zero Tolerance Policing in New York

The Police Commissioner of New York and other police commanders feel happy and proud at the success of their crime control measures. This became evident during interaction with them in the course of our visit to New York Police Headquarters and other police establishments of the city. There has been an unprecedented decrease of crime in New York. Over the past four years, crime in New York has dropped by 44 per cent and the Police Commissioner, Howard Safir, claims exultingly that New York has become the safest metropolis in the country.

Crime Statistics in New York

The 1993, New York City Mayor's Management Report lists many concrete improvements in the quality of life in New York City and Mayor Rudy Guiliani claims successful crime control as one of his biggest achievements. From 1993 to 1997 there has been a 60 per cent drop in murders and non-negligent homicides, 12.4 per cent drop in the number of rapes and 48 per cent drop in the number of robberies and burglaries. Guiliani points out that New York is responsible for a large share of overall crime reduction for the country as a whole. The citizens of New York feel that the streets of the city have become safer.

In 1993, there were 1946 murders committed in New York and many experts felt that the crime problem was intractable and almost ingrained in the culture of the city. This turnaround started during the incumbency of William Bratton as the Commissioner of Police, New York (from January, 1994 to April, 1996). He introduced "zero tolerance" policing and cracked on *squeegee men*: petty drug dealers, graffiti scribblers, and prostitutes who ruled the sidewalks in certain high crime neighbourhoods. He followed the approach advocated in "broken windows" theory of policing promoted by James P. Wilson. The "broken windows" theory holds that disorderly behaviour in public, if not firmly suppressed, will frighten citizens and encourage criminals and eventually lead to more serious crime problems. Conversely, serious crime problems can be quelled by mounting a large scale attack on petty crimes and disorderly behaviour through zero tolerance strategy.

Just as Rudy Guiliani had the good judgement to appoint Bratton as the Police Commissioner, Bratton had the good judgement to appoint Jack Maple, a brilliant police strategist, as his Deputy Commissioner incharge of crime control strategies. Bratton quickly introduced new management techniques and decentralised authority to give greater decision-making power to precinct and borough commanders. He integrated many of the police functions previously held by specialised units to empower patrol officers to deal with drug and gun crimes in the neighbourhoods they serve. This was indicative of a new shift in policing tactics. In traditional police organisation, it is presumed that those in higher ranks have greater wisdom and creativity and are able to take better decisions than the line officers. However, organisational development works in the early eighties by people like Tom Peters tried to change such old notions. Peters advocated that the executives should manage by walking with the line staff. He was of the view that men on the frontline possess "as many creative ideas on how to improve processes and find solutions to problems as top level managers."

Bratton had served earlier as the Chief of the New York Transit Police (the agency responsible for patrolling the city's vast subway system) and had carried out a large scale arrest of young New Yorkers for fare evasion and found that this had the effect of greatly reducing serious subway crime. He now introduced Compstat programmes as the main instrument for zero tolerance policing in New York City.

Compstat Program

Compstat program stands for computer statistics is based on mapping software that allows the chief of police and the local commanders to analyse crime data within 24 hours of the event. Compstat ensures that the supervisors at headquarters had the same information at the same time as the station commanders. Compstat meetings are now held twice a week and the precinct officers have to stand before the police chief and senior officers of the headquarters with a map of the territory on the screen over their heads and explain what they are doing to combat crime problems in their own areas. In the New York Police Department, technology is employed for electronic pin-mapping which facilitates visual portrayal of hot-spots and crime patterns. As stated by Bratton, "computer pin-mapping and crime analysis techniques are functioning as NYPD radar system, achieving early identification of crime patterns." While attending a Compstat session as the guest visitor of the Commissioner of Police, New York, I had the apprehension that Compstat strategy perhaps puts too much stress on police officers to show decline in crime. I was, however, assured by the New York police officers that constant vigil is kept to ensure that there is no suppression or minimization of crime.

Bratton also took the "handcuffs off" the police department and allowed patrol officers to stop and search citizens who were violating minor laws, to run warrant checks on them or question them about criminal activities in their neighbourhood. In his book *Turn Around* Bratton says that Compstat system is built on four concepts, namely, accurate and timely intelligence, rapid deployment of personnel and resources, effective tactics and relentless follow-up assessments.

There are sharp criticisms from the civil rights groups that aggressive zero tolerance policy has significantly increased abusive conduct and misuse of force on the part of the police. Amnesty International has reported that misconduct and abuse of authority by the police has increased sharply under the Guiliani administration's zero tolerance regime. The total number of citizen complaints filed annually with the Civilian Complaint Review Board (CCRB) has increased more than 60 per cent between 1992 and 1996.

In its 1998 mid-term report the CCRB has sharply criticised the New York Police and its Commissioner Howard Safir for dismissing substantiated complaints without apparent justification and failing to apprise the public as to his disposition of the complaints. It says: "Despite our repeated requests, the precise penalties of CCRB referrals resulting in guilty dispositions". Eighty-eight cases that the Board substantiated were dismissed by the police commissioner. It further took exception to a letter of the police commissioner to the executive director of NYCLU that the police misconduct complaints substantiated by the Board were not supported by an "appropriate level of evidence, as required by law."

However, violent crimes have been declining not only in New York but also in the USA as a whole. The National Crime Victimisation Survey crimes trends data (1973-96) published by the Bureau of Justice Statistics indicate that rapes have declined by 60 per cent from 1994 to 1996. Aggravated assaults declined by 27 per cent from 1993 to 1996. The victimisation data show that total violent crimes have come down by 19 per cent from 1994 to 1996 in the USA.

It is perhaps true that aggressive zero policing and other innovative police tactics had their definite impact on crime control in New York, but crime has declined in many other places in the USA, where different policing strategies and practices have been followed. Academics, criminologists and law-enforcement officials have advanced a number of theories for the steady decline of crime in the USA. They are of the view that no single factor or strategy has produced the drop in the crime rate. America's economic prosperity, low unemployment rates and demographic factors like decline of the crime-prone juveline segments of the population, huge increase in incarceration rates resulting from mandatory minimum dry laws, etc., are all causative factors behind this decline in crime.

The question before the law-enforcement officers is whether aggressive zero tolerance policing is the only way of effecting successful crime control. Sometimes 'get tough' measures leading to lengthy incarceration of a large number of young offenders may offer short-term relief, but in the long run by causing disruption of family ties and increasing levels of alienation, they may have negative consequences and prove to be crimogenic in themselves. There are reasons to fear that the success achieved by the New York police in reduction of crime will be undone if many citizens, and particularly the minority groups, feel that the police are becoming oppressive. The public support will then swing away. Bratton himself used to say that what is needed is not 'get tough' policing, but ‘get smart' policing.

13
Re-Examination of the Police Role in Crime Prevention

Today democratic countries all over the world is haunted by the spectre of crime and lawlessness. There is a sense of crisis about public security and at the centre of the crisis are the police who are to enforce laws and maintain order. There is a growing feeling among the members of the public that the police are unable to offer proper protection to the citizens and discharge their duties properly. In India, there are press reports everyday regarding soaring crime and the failure of the police to control it.

There is also demand from the police to provide them with more manpower and resources to deal with the rising crime graph. The police continually argue that if they are given more resources, especially personnel, they will be able to protect community against crime. This, according to many criminologists, is a myth. David Bayley has argued in his book *Police for the Future* that differences in crime rates cannot be attributed to variations in the number of police. In USA, the President's Commission on Law Enforcement and Administration of Justice pointed this out in 1967. For example, between 1970 and 1990, the number of full-time police officers in the United States rose by 70 per cent but the serious crimes rose by 78.8 per cent and violent crimes by 147 per cent. In Britain, between 1970 and 1990, police per capita rose by 12 per cent and crime rate by 67 per cent. In Canada, between 1970 and 1990, police per capita rose by 16 per cent and the crime rate by 34 per cent (the figures are taken from Prof. David Bayley's book *Police for the Future*).

There are also studies to show that even when the number of police has been reduced in some areas due to budgetary crisis or as a result of strikes, crime rates have remained unaffected. From my own experience I can say that during the police agitation in 1978 in Rourkella (where I was then posted as the Ranga DIG), policemen were not on the roads for nearly a week and we had to organize night patrolling through citizens' groups and Home Guards. However, there was no increase of crime during this period. Indeed, there was a decline.

The Audit Commission in Britain (1991), while summing up all the evidence before it, wrote recently "The terms of public debate need to move off the assumption that more police officers and police expenditures will lead to commensurate increase in the quantity and quality of police outputs". In war against crimes, sometimes Police Chiefs go on throwing more men into battles without any evidence that this will win the war. Knowledgeable and thoughtful people know the fact that the popular and prevalent notion that the efficiency or inefficiency of the police force is the decisive factor beyond increase or reduction of crime is erroneous. The capacity of the police to reduce and control crime is very much limited by social and economic forces over which they have not control. Police themselves also recognise this. And many thinking police officers complain that they are expected to protect the communities from the consequences of their own neglect. They see themselves as "a band-aid on cancer".

It is also becoming clear to police that they are gradually getting outgunned by circumstances. There is also growing realization that in the battle against crime, the police require active support and cooperation of the public. Empirical researches demonstrate arrests and better detection by the police, indicators of efficient police performance, do not have any significant impact in reduction of crime. It may sound strange but it is a fact that crime rate is not affected by the success of the police in solving crime.

Hence, a time has come when police leaders and administrators have to think of using police resources far more proactively for meeting the challenges of crime. Instead of spending of their energies reacting to crime, the police have to think of ways and means of preventing it. According to Ostrom Elaner, crime prevention is an activity in which the public must also be actively engaged. They must become co-producers of public safety.

For taking the challenge of crime prevention seriously, the police will have to break with many of the practices of the past and adopt new strategies. Consultation, adaptation, mobilization and problem solving are, according to David Bayley, some of the important elements of the new strategy. The police will have to evolve mechanisms for discussing crime prevention strategies with the members of the community by deepening contacts and holding regular meetings. This is happening in many of the democratic countries of the West. Since 1984, Britain has established over 200 Community Consultative Committees at the precinct level. The Canadian Mounted Police has also set-up Citizens Advisory Councils in all its detachments. These consultative committees enable the police to know of local needs and problems and the police often find out to their surprise that the people are concerned not only with serious crimes like murder, rape and robbery which are publicised in the media, but also with recurrent low-key troubles. Some of these issues can easily be settled quickly by the police with citizens' cooperation. Community meetings also enable members of the community to ventilate their grievances against the police and openly criticize some of the police officers for their acts of omission and commission. I attended a similar meeting in Birmingham during my visit to UK in the year 1996. The meeting enabled the citizens to ventilate their grievances against the police. Sometimes the police felt uncomfortable but they also tried to explain to the citizens what steps they have taken and plan to take in respect of various issues raised by the members of the public. The information made available by the citizens also enable the police to refine their operations.

Adaptation: There is also need for the police to adapt itself to the changing situations and circumstances. Instead of relying on some general policies and strategies formulated at Police Headquarters and to be applied and implemented force-wise, the local commanders should devise strategies to suit local needs. For effective crime prevention responsibility for formulating action plans has to be given to the frontline personnel. It has been aptly said that police organization allow enormous discretion in practice while at the same time maintaining a top-down command system. The formal and informal structure of authority in policing are not congruent. Sector policing in London, which has been started since 1991 tries to achieve the same goal. Police divisions are divided into two or three sectors. Each sector is under an Inspector who with his subordinate officers plans appropriate strategies for the sector in consultation with members of the local community. A radical proposal for real decentralization has now been put forward by the British Audit Commission, 1991. It recommends that decisions about security needs, strategies and resources will be made by the commanders of "Basic Police Units". The functions which have so long been monopolised by the headquarters of the Britain's 45 police forces should be given to the country's approximately 500 sub-divisions. Indeed, decentralization is the wave of the future. A time has come when in Indian Police we should also seriously think of decentralizing functions and give more power, authority and budgetary independence to the local commanders. In traditional police organizations, it is presumed that those in higher ranks have greater wisdom and creativity and are able to take better decisions than the line officers. However, organizational development works in the early 80s by people like Tom Peter tried to dispel such old notions. Peter pointed out that men on the frontline possess as many creative ideas on how to improve processes and find solutions to problems as top-level managers.

Mobilization: Further, Police also will have to increasingly mobilize the resources of the community to prevent crime. In many cities of USA, civilians are actively involved in intercepting and spotting criminal behaviour. The drivers of radio-equipped taxies, delivery-vans and telephone repair vehicles are sometimes trained to spot criminal activity and notify to the police. Volunteers wearing distinctive caps and arm-bands move in areas where criminal activity is likely to take place. In India, similar endeavours have been made occasionally, with some success, by energetic Police Chiefs. But I do not think if any sustained effort has been made to mobilize the resources of the community for the purpose of crime prevention. During my recent visit to Bangalore, I was happy to find that the Commissioner of Police Bangalore has started a help-line for rescue and rehabilitation of abandoned and neglected children. In this work, some of the well-known NGO groups as well as commercial firms have come forward to render help and assistance. Today, when most of the governments are facing financial crunch and there is enormous pressure on government budgets, substantial augmentation of police staff and resources will be expensive and difficult. Mobilization of the community can be one of the practical means of augmenting the crime focussed resources of the police.

There is also need for adopting a problem-solving approach which will enable the police along with the community to identify and address the real causes that lead to crime. This calls for a departure from the reactive incident-driven stance of the police. In America, Herman Goldstein developed the concept of problem-oriented policing which has encouraged the police to think somewhat differently about its role. Problem resolution, according to Goldstein, constitutes the true work of policing. It is seen that whenever there is a sharp rise in crime and disorder, the community wants the police to take strong and, if necessary, resort to extra legal methods. This is dishonest law enforcement which exploits public's fear of crime. Ultimately, dishonest law enforeement does not help because it does not tackle the true causes of crime and disorder.

Crime is a product of complex biological and social and economic conditions. Its prevention requires meaningful intervention after proper study and analysis. Public support is also essential. Law enforcement officers know that because the crime suspects are not identified readily, most of the crimes remain unsolved. Japan is an exception among the developed countries where the police solves about 58 per cent of the crimes. It is 21 percent in United States, even in respect of serious crimes. In Britain, the number is 35 per cent and in Canada 45 per cent. Success of police initiative to reduce crime is often determined by a factor outside police control. It is the time taken by victims and witnesses to notify the police.

It is true that mobilization of community support is not going to be an easy task in view of the alienation of the police from the community; but against the backdrop of growing crime and disorder the public will come forward to help the police only when the police is able to convince that the police also wants to help them.

14
Agony of Martin Massey: Lessons and Warnings

The brutal assault by the Delhi Police on Martin Massey, who inadvertently strayed into the road closed for the Prime Minister's motorcade, raises a number of issues worthpondering. It speaks of the growing organisational culture in the police which is totally devoid of any consideration for the rights and convenience of the common citizens. In a democratic society, the police should function as defenders of the rights of the citizens. Unfortunately, the main problem in India now is to police the police— *Quis custodiet ipsos custodes.*

It will be a serious mistake to view these incidents of police brutality and highhandedness as episodic aberrations of some rotten elements in the police force. Indeed, the roots of police deviance go much deeper. It basically spawns from an organisational culture that does not discourage or frown upon the abuse of authority and misuse of force. The culture that has grown up in the police for a variety of historical and political reasons is totally subservient to the political masters and lacks concern for the human rights of the citizens, particularly those belonging to the poor and downtrodden sections of the community. As a result, ideals and norms inculcated during the training period do not have any long-lasting impact on police officers. No qualitative transformation is effected.

People-friendly Policing

The senior police leaders must also share a major chunk of the responsibility for this brutalisation of the force. They have not taken sustained and well-conceived measures to educate and humanise the police force anywhere in the country. Efforts of some well-meaning officers in some areas have been a flash in the pan. In Great Britain, it was the two committed Commissioners of London Metropolitan Police, Mayne and Rowan, who were responsible for ushering in a new culture of people-friendly police which, despite some batterings in recent times, has made the British Police a beloved national institution. By turning a Nelson's eye to the police brutalities against inconvenient members of the society, the police leaders have encouraged a culture in which policemen revel in their unbridled exercise of authority and callously violate the rights of the citizens. The plain fact is forgotten that an alienated police believing in untrammeled use of authority and misuse of force cannot be good crime-fighters or law-enforcers. They can only be convenient 'hand maidens' for their political masters an instrument for abuse and misuse.

Massey's plight also highlights the obstrusively paranoiac VIP security arrangements which cause serious inconvenience and harassment to the common man. Motorcades of the Prime Minister or the President regularly block traffic movements on the much frequented roads. Even pedestrians' movement is halted for a period that may extend up to half an hour. However, there are no two opinions on the issue that in the prevailing security senario some of the VVIPs face real threats and their security arrangements have to be streamlined as well as strengthened. Unfortunately, at present, we are sacrificing the quality of VIP security cover through needlessly elaborate, and at times unimaginative, security arrangements.

VIP Security Duties

Many of the officers and men deployed for VIP security duties are untrained and uninitiated for these special tasks and by their intrusive and arrogant conduct cause lasting resentment in the people's minds. Common people are appalled by the spectacle of VIPs, and at times even their sons and daughters, going for shopping or to attend social and cultural functions accompanied by gun-totting policemen or commandoes. This has become a kind of a status symbol. Many of our VVIPs lack the sensitivity to understand and appreciate the disgust and revulsion as also needless trouble it causes to fellow citizens. If they are so scared and tizzy, they should not attend social and cultural functions. People occupying important places in public life should brave certain risks. Otherwise, they should withdraw themselves from public life. Further, on a couple of occasions I have shared the disgusting experience of passengers travelling by air feel on the unnecessary delay when the airport is closed 45 minutes before a VIP flight takes off or lands. Aircrafts have to either circle in the air or are diverted to some nearby airports.

I have had the opportunity of seeing how in many Western countries VIP security arrangements, though meticulously planned, are almost invisible. In countries like England, Sweden, Denmark, members of the royalty move about without their presence causing the least inconvenience to the ordinary citizens. The basic fact is often forgotten that a hostile public will only make the success of VIP security arrangements more difficult.

Therefore, the time has come to examine if the proliferation in the number of VIPs, and the scale and category of their security arrangements, are justified by the realities of the threat perception. Very often such threat perceptions are illusory. The Ministry of Home Affairs has informed the National Human Rights Commission that such a review exercise has been undertaken. One hopes that this review will be done realistically and drastically to reduce the number of VIPs really needing gun-wielding security personnel which in turn will save huge sums of money to the exchequer. Attempts made earlier by the Home Minister to reduce the number of VIPs in 'Z' category security had to be abandoned in the face of howls of protests from the affected VIPs.

Today in Delhi thousands of policemen are deployed for VIP security duties. Many of them are ill-trained with slow reflexes and responses. As the VIP security job is hazardous, men deployed on security duties must possess a heightened sense of awareness of the dangers lurking round. Further, to be effective, they must be as inconspicuous as possible. A careful review is necessary by the security experts to assess the present VIP security arrangements against the background of public inconvenience and the lack of professionalism and perceptiveness of the security staff.

15
Criminal Investigation—Myth and Reality

Reports have appeared in different newspapers regarding the detection of the criminals involved in the murder case of the 'Outlook' magazine's cartoonist Irfan Hussain by the Delhi Police. The police claim that the confessions of the accused persons have provided clues to the solution of three or four other cases of serious crime. Some of the newspaper correspondents have questioned the claim of the police to detect a sensational case just on the basis of confession of the suspects. In this connection, it is good to dispel the impression prevailing in public mind that only through patient and painstaking investigation, the police work out the clues and crack difficult cases. This, however, as many law-enforcement officers know, is not true. Films and novels portray that only through tireless, unglamorous but professional hard work the investigators succeed in the detection of cases. They have like Sherlock Holmes an open mind, and investigation work becomes a battle of wits between a devilishly clever criminal and an equally ingenious detective.

The reality of criminal investigation work, however, is very different. Very often the successes are not the result of dogged detective work. Cleared crimes tend to solve themselves. The perpetrator is either known (and in some cases present when the police officer first arrives) or can be identified through the information supplied by the victim or some witnesses. In USA, the President's Crime Commission scrutinized 1905 cases examined by Los Angeles Police during a typical period. In 350 cases where the suspect could be identified the police were able to clear 86 per cent of those crimes. In the remaining 1556 cases, where no suspect could be quickly identified, the police clearance was only 12 per cent.

In the police world, there is a basic division of criminal cases according to named and unnamed suspects. Detectives know if the perpetrators of crime are not identified quickly, it becomes difficult to find the criminals on their own. Nor is physical evidence important, as David Bayley says in his book *Police for the Future* (page 27), in determining if the case is to be pursued. Physical evidence goes to support the testimony that identifies the suspects. It is seldom used diagnostically to trace out the suspects. In cases of burglary and robbery the police often carefully look at different objects in the scene of crime and "dust" them to find out finger-prints. But they often laugh among themselves at the futility of this public relations exercise. Indeed, the fact of the matter is that the criminal investigators begin with an identification and then collect evidence; they rarely collect evidence and then make an identification. Thus, the chances of solving a crime do vary with the nature of the crime. There are higher rates of detection in cases of confrontational crimes and lower rates for property crimes. The four interpersonal crimes (murder, assault, rape and robbery) have high clearance rates because very often the victims or some witnesses have seen the suspects.

On the other hand, property crimes like burglary, theft, arson, etc. afford no opportunity for the victims to identify the offender. Most of them are 'cold crimes', the offender is long gone by the time police arrive. In USA, the police solve 45 per cent of the violent crimes against 18 per cent of property crimes. Detection rates in homicide cases are 67 per cent while motor vehicle theft cases only 18 percent (figures of rate of detection in India are to be given). Thus, the solvability of crimes is built into the crimes themselves. Even the most determined detective work is not going to change that fact of life.

Investigators have to spend long hours in interrogating people strongly suspected to be involved in the commission of crimes in an attempt to get them confess Confession, as a Japanese training manual puts it, "is the king". However, a person, as enjoined by law cannot be convicted solely on the basis of his conviction. Hence confession should help the investigators in collecting evidence needed for successful prosecution. Unfortunately in India in many cases the police by force or threat obtain confessions which are invalid in law, and then do not systematically and legally collect the evidence disclosed by the confession. This results in acquittal in a large number of cases. Hence, a good investigating officer must be well conversant with the rules and laws of evidence. There are investigators who are keen and painstaking, but all their endeavour often goes in vain because evidence collected by them may not be of use to the prosecuting officer or to the court.

Police detectives also work hard to get 'secondary clearances'. The secondary clearance occurs when a person who is prosecuted or at times convicted for one crime confesses to the commission of other crime. The criminals nabbed in Irfan Hussain's case are reportedly confessing that they have committed few more murders. This will help detection of those cases by the police. In this connection it may be mentioned that studies done in United States and Great Britain indicate that the only way for the police to improve detection of cases is to pay greater attention to obtain secondary clearances. Once again the point to note is that the ability of the police to solve crimes depends on having a reasonable suspicion about the likely culprits.

In police investigation emphasis is given to the 'mystique of finger-prints'. In reality, however, finger-prints rarely solve crimes because of the difficulty of getting useable finger-prints from a crime scene. Finger-prints are of use in confirming the identity of a suspect who is in custody. It helps the prosecution to nail down the case. But the problem is that the finger-prints are of little use in identifying a suspect in the first place. Samuel Walker (Sense and Non-sense about Crime) says that when their own homes are burglarized, many detectives refuse to allow the finger-print technicians in. They know from experience that the process "really produces a useable print and only leaves a big mess". However, DNA identification procedures may change the situation. DNA technology now considerably enhances the ability of the police to identify the criminals from the physical clues left at the scene of crime.

In police operations there is also considerable emphasis on quick response. It is generally believed that rapid response from the police would enable it to catch more criminals and detect more cases. In USA, the President's Crime Commission also supported this idea. Recent studies by the criminologists, however, show that so far most crimes are concerned, the police response time is irrelevant. About two-thirds of the cases registered by the police in India are 'cold crimes' where the criminal is long gone before the crime is discovered. Nevertheless there are few crime situations where response time may matter like commercial robberies. If a witness is able to inform the police while the crime is taking place, the quick arrival of the police on the scene of crime improves the chances of detection.

Studies on the other hand have shown that very often the critical delay is the time taken by the victim or witnesses to call the police. A Kansas city study done by the President's Commission on Law-Enforcement and Administration of Justice (1980) found that victims took about six minutes time to call the police. About half the victims talked to someone else first before calling the police, and many decided not even to call the police. In India many people do not report crimes to the police and those who report also do so after considerable delay. A powerful 'avoidance syndrome' is at work.

Further, because of the pressure of miscellaneous duties like VIP visits, law and order problems the police do not give more than 30 per cent (as revealed in a study of the National Police Commission) of their time for investigation of cases. Quality and standard of investigating officers of the State CID is better as they are not burdened with other miscellaneous duties. However, the amount of attention given to the investigation of a case or the manner in which the police force is organized for investigation does not affect clearance rates. Inherent solvability phenomenon is a factor that seriously affects the outcome of cases. And the critical ingredient in solving the crime is whether the public, victims and witnesses, provide information to the police that help it to identify the suspects. A study of criminal investigation by Rand Corporation indicated that while some of the police department in USA do a poor job of handling evidence (collecting irrelevant and inadmissible evidence) either due to lack of knowledge or out of ulterior motives, the police departments with improved training programmes and better procedures did not have higher clearance rates.

For detection of crimes targetting of career criminals is one of the important strategies of the police, well-known criminologist Wolfgang and his colleagues in one of the most influential studies concluded that a small portion of known offenders commit a disproportionate amount of crime. Theoretically, a 'selective incapacitation' of the known offenders would result in a significant reduction in crime. However, evaluation of Repeat Offender Project (ROP) or 'Perpetrator-oriented Patrol' (POP) in some of the American cities yielded unsatisfactory results. It was found that such programmes were 'unproductive' and 'time-consuming'.

Section-III

16

Training for Transformation

Training has been defined as a conscious effort to improve and increase knowledge, skill and aptitude of an individual in a desired direction. The object of training is not only to develop the professional skill of an individual for the performance of duties in an assigned job, but also to improve his capacity for shouldering greater responsibility. Unfortunately, though the crucial and transforming role of training is acknowledged by one and all, there has not been any sustainable and meaningful endeavour to improve the scope and quality of police training in the country.

This is a pity because the police was the first civil service in the country to think of systematic institutional training for its personnel. A training school for constables was first established in Vellore (Madras Presidency) in 1859. Similar training institutions were set up in Phillore (Punjab) and Moradabad (U.P.) in the early 1890s. Police training schools were established in the first decade of the century in most of the provinces for the training of officers of and above the rank of sub-inspectors as a result of recommendations of the All India Police Commission of 1902-03.

Unfortunately, police training was patterned on the training given in military training establishments. The military model was accepted by police training institutions due to historic reasons and circumstances. The senior ranks of the police services in the second half of the last century, when police training institutions came into being, were filled by officers taken from the British Indian Army. While organising training on the model of the army, the fact that the police and army had different roles to perform and work in different environments was not taken into consideration.

The same trend continued even after Independence. In 1971, the Government of India set up a committee on police training under the chairmanship of eminent sociologist and educationist, M.S. Gore. The committee reviewed the existing facilities in different training institutions and came to the unflattering conclusion that police training had been badly neglected over the years and training arrangements, except in some central organisations, were unsatisfactory both quantitatively and qualitatively.

The committee in an able report made some well thought out recommendations for improving the training syllabi, organisation of training and instructional methods and so on. The committee also expressed the view that the most important reason for this unhappy situation was a lack of conviction about the value of training on the part of the administration, including the higher ranks of police services. The Gore Committee rightly shifted the focus of the training from drill and regimentation to the development of proper attitudes through the study of social and behavioural science and modern management norms and techniques.

Many of the important recommendations of the Gore Committee were accepted by the government and some concrete steps were taken to tone up the functioning of the important police and paramilitary training institutions of the central government. Unfortunately, the quality and the nature of the police training in many of the states have not registered any improvement after nearly three decades since the publication of the report. Training has remained, as described in the report of the Gore Committee, 'a ritual where unwilling and ill-equipped instructors are performing the rites of training and drilling to the unwilling trainees.'

It is now recognised that no worthwhile improvement in the training of police personnel is possible unless capable and conscientious officers are brought in to the training institutions as trainers. The trainer must enjoy an honoured position in the institution so that he can play the role of a change agent. If the training is to serve the primary purpose of preparing an individual to meet the challenges of today and complexities of the future, the role of the instructor as the change agent is crucial. The Gore Committee recommended suitable incentives including rent free accommodation, special pay, recognition in the form of subsequent promotions or good postings for the trainers with a view to attracting the best available talent.

Unfortunately, except in some central training institutions, these incentives have not been made available to the trainers. As a result, competent and qualified staff are loath to come as trainers in the police training schools/colleges. Very often, postings in the training institutions are viewed as a punishment. At present there is no fixed tenure of the trainers and many of the officers posted in the training institutions unabashedly continue their efforts to get out as speedily as possible. There is no planned turnover of staff and consequently no infusion of new blood. Many of the trainers are without any specialized training or knowledge to the subject which they are supposed to teach. In some of the institutions, the trainers receive no evaluation of their capabilities as there is no feedback system.

As Director of the National Police Academy, I visited different police training institutions in the UK. I found that, unlike in India, the job of trainers in police training institutions was a prestigious one and there was a long list of officers willing to serve. Trainers not only had excellent teaching and communication skills, but also wide ranging police experience. They, thus, brought into the training process the necessary wisdom and experience to bridge the gap between theory and practice.

There is also a need to change the methodology of training. Instruction in the police training schools and colleges is largely based on the lecture method. There is an acute paucity of good training materials and aids. Very few good films have been produced in India on police training. Today, in all well-known institutions, there have been important changes in the methods of instruction. Classroom instruction and discussions are accompanied by a number of role-play scenarios. The prevailing philosophy is to get the trainees to perform as soon as possible to reinforce what they have learnt. The important point is that the police training institution is a professional institution where it is necessary to impart to the trainees not merely knowledge of the subjects but also to learn how this knowledge can be applied to the work they will be required to perform in the field.

Further, most police training institutions have no research base. The Gore Committee was struck by the total absence of any research facilities in any police training institution. The situation has not changed since then. Research is absolutely necessary so that trainees remain intellectually vibrant and up-to-date in their knowledge. Fundamental research may not always be possible in such institutions but some amount of applied research by the instructional staff to remove the hiatus between theoretical training and practical police work is critical. Without a research cell under competent instructors it is impossible for the training institutions to take note of the changing situations and develop realistic training programmes. And, to survive successfully in today's changing and dynamic world, law enforcement officers have to be continually updated on the latest techniques and developments in policing.

In most of the police training institutions there is no system of evaluation. Evaluation is, however, essential for a dynamic training system. The Gore Committee strongly recommended the importance of developing a sound evaluation system in police training in the following words: 'In order to ensure that trainees are developing properly, a system of evaluation which can serve as the basis of further improvement in teaching as well as learning should be introduced. It should be continuous and comprehensive enough to cover both the academic and non-academic areas and related to the objectives of the training programmes.'

A study conducted by the National Police Academy on evaluation practices in vogue (some of the police training colleges were randomly selected for the study) showed that in seven out of nine police training institutions, the trainees' reactions to the training programmes were not evaluated by adopting any well-laid-out scheme. Syllabi in the training institutions were found to be fixed and evaluation did not play any role in the modification of various syllabi. Informal evaluation procedures suggested by the Gore Committee, namely question-answer sessions, group discussions and role playing were not part of the training module.

Often, a noteworthy feature of police training is its isolation, an unfortunate foretelling of the isolation that is characteristic of police life in service. Like in a military college or other 'total institutions', the recruit is placed in a circumstance of new social dependencies and resocialized. The isolation begins in the training establishments where the recruit is immersed into a new environment requiring total commitment, conformity and loyalty. To counteract this isolation, police training should be broadened with a view to developing in police officers a better understanding of their role in relation to total societal goals and better understanding of the behaviour of particular groups.

The ultimate success of any training programme is dependent upon a wise and dynamic recruitment policy. Training, to an extent, can make up for some deficiencies in the recruit, as one experienced officer has put it, but it cannot rectify the original error. If recruits of poor quality are enlisted because of extraneous considerations, no amount of training can mould them into competent and capable officers. At present, because of age relaxation, recruits of higher age groups are entering the various ranks of the police. As the Director of the National Police Academy, I had written to the MHA that IPS trainees of a higher age group (at present the upper age limit is 28 instead of 24 in the past) find it difficult to cope with the stress and strain imposed by a rigorous training programme. Some of them arrive with frozen attitudes and a negative approach emphasized during the training. I strongly advocated that the IPS probationers should be caught young, within the age bracket of 20 to 24 at the time of recruitment.

The twenty-first century is fast approaching. Vast and sweeping alterations are taking place which will radically affect the role performance of the police. With rapid industrialization, urbanization and operation of other crimogenic factors, there will be a steep increase in crime. By the end of the century, India's population may reach the billion mark. An expert estimate is that the country will be faced with a forbiding challenge of crime to the tune of eight million offences under the Indian Penal Code and about 20 million under special acts and laws. The face of crime is also changing. In tomorrows diverse and protean society, police officers will be called upon to deal with crimes as varied as computer fraud, nuclear terrorism, trafficking in narcotics and so on.

The disruptive and secessionist elements are active in various parts of the country. The police force has not only to be mentally alert, but also physically tough. In police training there must be a balance of both indoor and outdoor aspects of the job. It is necessary to place a substantial degree of emphasis on physical fitness, survival training and judgmental shooting. The police personnel have to test their judgement and accuracy in 'shoot'/'don't shoot' situations, which will prepare them to face situations when confronted with a decision whether or not to use deadly force.

However, it has to be borne in mind that the effectiveness of today's law enforcement officers must be based not only on their knowledge, skills and abilities, but on the ethical application of what they have learned. In his book, *Character and Cops: Ethics in Policing,* Edwin Delattre aptly said: 'What is taught by the academies about ideals should be woven into the realities of the streets.' Police officers have to be motivated by a value system. Otherwise, skills learnt may be misused or not sustained.

Often, there are allegations against the police (some not without substance) of gross violations of human rights. The Constitution of India has laid great stress on human rights and dignity. The Supreme Court, in a memorable judgement, in the case of D.K. Basu *vs.* State of Bengal, stated: 'whenever the human dignity is wounded, civilization takes a step backward. The flag of humanity on each such occasion must fly at halfmast.' During training, the point has to be stressed that adherence to human rights norms will enable the police to discharge its legal functions more effectively and competently. It will also help the police to build better and stronger bridges with the community.

Without support of the community, the police cannot function properly. For effective crime prevention and order maintenance, support of the community is a *sine qua non.* The Council of Europe set up a committee of experts for the promotion of information and education in the field of human rights. The committee selected the police member states as the primary target for the attainment of its objectives and laid utmost emphasis on the teaching of human rights in police training. Its book, *Human Rights and Police,* stressed that police officers should be carefully selected for their human qualities and properly trained to perform their duties in an ethically correct manner.

For effecting any real improvement in police work on the ground there should be the utmost stress on training of police personnel. However, training, though essential, is not the only input for improving and optimizing work performance and effecting attitudinal transformation of the officers and men. Training can be effective, provided the organisation has faith in it and the organisational climate encourages the observance of precepts taught during training. A heavy responsibility rests on the senior officers to build a congenial organisational climate.

17
Role of Trainers in Police Training Institution

The first and foremost requirements of good training institution is to have good trainers. The trainer does play the role of a change agent in the organisation. "If training is to serve the primary purpose of preparing an individual to meet the challenges of today and complexities of the future, if training is to help in heralding suitable changes in the organisation so that it remains a living organism", says the Report of the Committee on Police Training set up by the Government of India under the chairmanship of Prof. M.S. Gore in 1971, "the role of the instructor as the change agent is crucial". It goes without saying that officers of proven integrity and ability should be chosen as trainers in any training institution. Unfortunately, many of the police training institutions have become dumping-grounds for officers who are not required elsewhere. Such officers spread the message of cynicism and disillusionment in the training institutions and shape the outlook and approach of the trainees in a negative manner. Heads of many police forces are reluctant to spare capable officers from field duties out of the mistaken fear that the effectiveness of the force will be adversely affected if they are allowed to merely take on a teaching role. On the other hand, assigning teaching role to dynamic and forward-looking officers will have a beneficial impact on the police organisation in the long run. Policemen trained by them will eventually improve the overall effectiveness of the force.

Qualities of a Good Trainer

A successful instructor must possess certain qualities. The first and foremost requirement of a good instructor is that he should have a thorough professional knowledge and experience of the subject which he is to teach along with transparent sincerity and enthusiasm for the job. Preparing a detailed lesson plan will have to be an article of faith with the instructors. Young trainees will be inspired by the trainers' enthusiasm and conscientiousness. A good trainer must pay proper attention to his dress and appearance. His bearing and appearance must display self-confidence and vitality. The manner of presentation is also equally important. A calm and clear voice and not shouting actually helps. The trainer should be supportive and non-threatening. The tone of his voice, his non-verbal expressions, should make the learners comfortable and encourage them to raise questions, offer suggestions. A trainer must also possess adequate empathy. This is the ability to put oneself in the shoes of others and the facility to recognise the fears and uncertainties in the minds of the trainees when learning additional skills and techniques. Empathy enables a trainer to point out personal difficulties encountered by him in similar learning situations with a view to putting the trainees at ease.

Exposition of the trainer must be clear and to the point. He must present his subject in a simple language and logical sequence and not use too many jargons and cliches. He must give his attention not only to those occupying the front benches but to the entire class. Each pupil should feel that the teacher's attention is on him and he, in his turn, must do his share.

Recapitulation

The pace of presentation of the talk must not be quick. It is better to move slowly than to push for rapid and sloppy completion. There should be plenty of recapitulation and free use of illustrations and examples drawn particularly from his own experience. Plenty of questions should be asked to ascertain if the trainees have understood properly all the points in the exposition. Questions are asked not only to test the knowledge but also to generate interest. It also tests the learners' ability to utilise their knowledge. Questions should be distributed evenly and no section of the class should be ignored. Questions should be clear and not ambiguous. It is better to avoid repetition of the questions. Otherwise, the class will develop the habit of not paying attention when the questions are first asked. Again if a teacher finds that his pupils are becoming inattentive, he should immediately shoot questions at them. The instructor need not always accept the first correct answer. He should refer it back to the class and class can be asked if the answer is correct or if anyone disagrees with it. If an answer is partially correct, it should be used as a means of asking the students to think more on the subject. A sure sign of good teaching is the interest it generates in the class and the level of interest is indicated by the manner of questions that are being posed.

Listening Skill

A good trainer conscientiously moves the group of learners to a pre-set destination. There may be stops and shifts, but the eye is always fixed on certain standards and levels. The trainer must also be a good listener. He must carefully hear the questions raised by the trainees and try to understand if they reflect some other problems which have not been highlighted. He must assume the posture of a careful listener when questions are asked and maintain an eye contact with the questioner. The trainer must cultivate a sense of humour. A talk laced with subdued humour becomes interesting and captures the attention of the entire class.

Impartial

An instructor must be just and must, on no account, display favouritism. It is likely that an instructor may like some trainees a little more than others, but he has to be extra-careful so that he does not display favouritism in any way in dealing with the trainees. The pupils should not get an impression that some are 'more equals than others'.

Adult Learning

Besides possessing communication skill, a good trainer should have flexibility in approach, role versatility and capability of inspiring and energising the listeners. The participatory-training programme will lose its meaning unless it is flexible and open. Police trainers have to impart training to the adults who have their own speed of perception, assimilation and retention. The trainers must understand the psychology of adult learning. Often adults are resistant to change because of their desire to retain the status-quo and incapacity to see the need for change. They also tend to develop set and frozen attitudes. The trainers have to understand this and apply some simple rules of adult learning. They have to remember that adult learning is aided by active practice rather than passive reception. Adult learning becomes easier when the message draws on the prior experience of the adults. Motivation, reinforcement and participation are important factors of adult learning. Unfortunately, it is found that the majority of trainers posted in training institutions are not themselves trained in the art of instruction and unaware of the various instructional methods and aids. In the SVP National Police Academy, Training of Trainers' Course is being organised regularly to build up the capabilities of police trainers in the preparation of training designs, identification of training needs, developing tools for evaluating the effectiveness of training programmes. I have found that these Courses for the Training of Trainers and Training of Administrators of training institutions have been quite successful and the participants felt that they are going back enriched with new methods and techniques and ideas for police training.

Self-Development

The trainer also must be keen for self-development. The development of self is not merely to develop cognitively, and acquire new concepts and new information, but also emotional development, sensitivity to one's reactions and sensitivity to others. In the conventional training methodology the trainer needs to be merely an expert on the content. Only the cognitive development of the trainer is emphasised. Self and the emotionaly/sensory development of the trainer is not even mentioned. However, the trainer must understand his strength and weaknesses, concerns and anxieties and this understanding of self will become the basis of his understanding others. The trainer must also know his development tasks and roles. He must go through the development process himself and then alone he will understand how others do so. It is also desirable for the trainer to have awareness of group dynamics and the dynamics of trainer-trainee relationship. He must be aware of underlying dynamics that effects individual and group learning and understand issues that need monitoring. Unfortunately, in many of the police training institutions trainers are not able to come in close contact with the trainees as the number of trainees is very large. If the interaction is not close and continuous, personal and social qualities of the trainees cannot be properly evaluated.

Role Model

The trainer has to project himself as a role model. Participants learn by emulating the model presented by the trainers. The direct use of self as a model is crucial in any participatory training. For example, if participants have displayed great physical stamina and high levels of energy in any programme the trainer has to demonstrate his physical stamina and energy throughout the programme.

Counsellor

The trainer also plays an important role as the counsellor who should guide individual trainees during periods of stress and strain and help the trainees to assess their potentiality and personal competencies with a view to enabling them to reflect, grow and change. He must show genuine interest in the growth of the trainees and organise special sessions to enhance self-confidence and self-esteem of some of the trainees who are found somewhat deficient.

Congruence

A trainer, in order to be successful, has to be facilitative. A stand-off trainer's role per se is one of the authority, power and ego gratification. This has to be constantly balanced by humility, humour and perspective. It is vital for him to develop an attitude of respect for the learning and experience of the trainees. If the trainer projects himself as an omniscient expert, resistance is bound to brew. A trainer has to remember that his carefully prepared lectures will soon be forgotten, trainees will remember his attitudes and behaviours. Carl Rogers and others have identified congruence as the key quality in effective communicators. Congruence is also essential for the success of a facilitative trainer. A trainer can be effective if he acts in accordance with the concepts presented by him in the classroom.

Evaluation

All training programmes must have a system of evaluation of instructors. The trainer himself must evolve a system of receiving feed-back from the trainees and, wherever possible, an assessment from his colleagues. However, the responsibility for assessing the effectiveness of an individual instructor should be mainly with the head of the training institution. It will be necessary for the latter to discuss with each instructor the lesson plan prepared by him, the methodology he has proposed and the integration of instructional aids in the teaching process that he has planned. It will be necessasry for the head of the institution to visit the classrooms occasionally and assess the reactions of trainees to different instructors.

Nevertheless, the success of an instructor will largely depend upon organisational climate. Even the most proficient instructor will not be successful unless he receives support and encouragement from the senior officers, and particularly the head of the training institution. "The lack of conviction about the value of training on the part of administration including the higher ranks of the police service", as Gore Committee puts it, "remains a major inhibiting factor in the development of the instructional staff".

Section-IV

18
Features of Modern Terrorism

The Encyclopaedia of Social Science has defined terrorism as a term used to describe the method, or theory behind the method, whereby an organized group or party seeks to achieve its avowed aim through the systematic use of violence. Terrorism implies striking terror in the hearts of those against whom it is applied. Brian Jenkins, an acknowledged authority on terrorism, calls it "Violence for effect". The U.S. State Department's *Annual Survey Patterns of Global Terrorism, 1983* defined terrorism as "premeditated, politically motivated violence perpetrated against non-combatant targets by sub-national groups or clandestine state agents". International terrorism is terrorism involving the territory or citizens of more than one country and has been defined in a publication of the C.I.A. as the "threat or use of violence for political purposes when such action is intended to influence the attitude and behaviour of a target group other than its immediated victim and its ramifications transcend national boundaries".

Unpredictability

Terrorism is frightening because the violence unleashed by the terrorists is unpredictable. Terrorist violence can occur at any time and anywhere. This unpredictability magnifies the effect of terrorism's violence and makes it difficult to combat. Studies of the victims of air raids during the Second World War, have shown that extreme helplessness caused by the unpredictability of the danger caused acute distress among the citizens and shook the belief "it would not happen to me". This unpredictability of the danger which as a psychologically damaging factor is very much amenable to manipulation by the terrorists.

Symbolic Targets

Violence of the terrorists is also not mindless. Terrorists choose symbolic targets. The targets are chosen because their identity or location or activities symbolize something which the terrorists will like to attack. Israeli athletes were attacked at the 1972 Olymipic games in Munich by the Palestinians who wanted to strike out at Israel. In 1977 the Red Army faction kidnapped and murdered German industrialist Hans Martin Schleyer because he was viewed as the symbol of western capitalism. Egyptian President Anwar Sadat was assassinated because he symbolized Arab reconciliation with the State of Israel. The symbolism attached to the terrorists' victim may be personal (Margaret Thatcher and the I.R.A.) or representative, or it may be 'everyman' symbolism.

Anyone in an American or Indian jet or in a Jewish house of worship can be singled out as the object of attack by the terrorists. Compassion and ethical considerations in the past did exert some influence on the operations of therrorists and they refrained from indulging in indiscriminate killings. Russian terrorists of Nardonaya volya or Indian terrorists in the past tried to avoid the killing of women and children. These moral scruples do not weigh at all with contemporary terrorists who are turning into cold-blooded liquidationists for whom there are no 'innocents'. The object of the terrorists in killing innocent men, whose death can be of no value to their cause, is to disorient a large section of the population by showing that the government is not able to provide safety and security to its citizen and thus perform one of its basic functions. There is, therefore, a significant shift in the ideological under-pinnings of contemporary terrorist groups. A growing element of nihilism is becoming evident in their operations. A growing number of terrorist groups are non-ideologically motivated, appealing to no specific constituency on whose behalf they claim to act. Only activism gives meaning to their empty lives. As a result, terrorism often degenerates into motiveless violence.

"The less clear the political purpose, the greater its appeal to unbalanced persons. The motives of men fighting a cruel tyranny are different from those of rebels against a democratically elected government".

"Terrorism" by Walter Laqueur

U.N. Definition

The United Nations has been trying for years to arrive at a satisfactory definition of terrorism. This has not been possible because of political differences and divergent perceptions among the different states. We are living in a world in which some states condemn terrorism, while states that use terrorism to govern or as an instrument of foreign policy often refuse to acknowledge their participation in terrorism. The debates that revolve round the application of terrorism and the value judgments that accompany the concept further increase the complexity of terrorism. Terrorism creates ethical dilemmas for individuals as well as nations because it combines the struggle for power and freedom, heroic self-sacrifice, with ruthless and callous disregard for human lives.

Terrorism and Insurgency

Often terrorism is confused with insurgency. There are, however, some major differences between the two. Terrorism is usually the weapon of a small group, but insurgency enjoys a far greater volume of mass support. Because the terrorists constitute a small group, they do not try to establish control over any territory or run a government. Insurgents, on the other hand, try to replace the old regime with one of its own seeking. The endeavour of the insurgents is to enlarge and expand the base they will govern as models which will attract the population and convert them to their cause.

Media Relationship

Another essential requirement of terrorism is publicity. News media attention is necessary to spread the world of terrorist violence to a much wider audience. It is aptly said that there is some kind of a symbiotic relationship between terrorisn and the media. The terrorists rely on the media to give publicity to their terror-inspiring goals, and the media, in their turn, view the acts of the terrorists as rewarding news items. The media enhance the power image of the terrorist groups and give them a larger-than-life appearance. Using terror is a low-cost, high-result route to a world-audience. Widespread publicity of terror-violence through the media engenders a climate of intimidation which affects the quality of life in a society and ultimately destabilizes its social institutions. Further, extensive coverage of incidents of terror by the media dulls the general public's sense of opprobrium and heightens the public's acceptance of terror-violence as a fact of life. Walter Laqueur has very appropriately said.

"The media are the terrorists' best friend. The terrorist act by itself is nothing; publicity is all".

Flexibility

Another unique feature of terrorism is its flexibility. Anyone can use it and anyone can be its target. Wars between states are confined to geographical areas and have a declared set of combatants, but terrorism can be conducted with relative ease across many national borders. Brian

Jenkins has pointed out that today many governments are using terrorist groups as an arm of their foreign policy. Thus terrorism has emerged as some sort of a 'surrogate warfare'. Nations unable to mount a conventional military challenge have looked upon terrorism as an alternative and thus it has emerged as a standard aspect of armed conflict among nations. Terrorism is becoming an accepted political instrument and many state governments tolerate and even exploit terrorism in the manner that European powers in the 17th and 18th centuries combated, and also exploited, Mediterranean piracy. Actually, in this nuclear age, even the superpowers like the United States and the old Soviet Union have found that it is sometimes safer to compete by backing terrorist groups because that is an effective low-risk operation. Thus terrorism will continue to be a difficult and persistent feature of international violence with no remedies or fool-proof defences on the horizon. Conflicting interests of nation states will make universal counter-measures impossible.

Difference with State Terror

It is argued by some that terrorism and state terror are only two sides of the same coin. But state terror is far more sinister and the actual number of incident and victims involved in state terrorism far outweigh the toll of terrorism. State terror amounts to an abuse of legitimate power available to the state for legitimate purposes of national defence and state security. Terrorists commit acts of public terror while concealing their real identity. The state, on the other hand, commits acts of secret terror directed against its knowns opponents. Terrorism is a war of attrition fought by an invisible but vocal army. The state has no reason to act by attrition. It can exercise its will immediately. State terror, however, can be the breeding-ground for terrorism or its military cousin, guerrilla warfare. State terrorism has become today a global phenomenon, confined to no particular ideology or location. State terrorism intimidates whole groups and sometimes whole nations and the remedy has to come from outside sources. In view of the sheer scale of crimes and mass terror that have been and are being committed by modern tyrannies, there should be no doubt that state terror poses a far more intractable problem for humanity than the containment and reduction of factional terror. The international community today finds itself ill-equipped to combat this form of terrorism.

Varieties of Terrorism

P. Wilkinson, in *Political Terrorism* draws a distinction between four types of terrorisn-criminal, psychic, war and political terrorism.

Criminal terrorism is the systematic use of terror for ends of material gain. Psychic terrorism, on the other hand, has religious or mystical ends. The aim of war terrorism is to diminish the resistance of the enemy and reduce his ability to fight with the ultimate object of destroying him. Political terrorism is defined as the systematic use or threat of violence to secure political goals.

Wilkinson further divides political terrorism under the following categories: (a) Revolutionary terrorism (b) Repressive terrorism. Revolutionary terrorism is systematic tactics of terrorism with the objective of bringing about political revolution. Revolutionary terrorism is a part of a revolutionary strategy and manifests itself in socially and politically unacceptable violence. There is also a pattern of symbolic selection of the victims of terrorism. Repressive terrorism, on the other hand, is use of terrorist violence for the purpose of suppressing or restraining certain groups or forms of behaviour considered undesirable by the oppressor.

Urban Drift

Another important trend in contemporary terrorism is that urban terrorism is supplanting more and more rural guerrilla tactics. Following the failure of the rural-based revolutionary attempts in South America, an urban drift has become clearly evident in various contemporary terrorist operations. Urban-based terrorism has become the order of the day.

Drug and Terror

Terrorists require a good deal of money for carrying out their operations. Terrorist movements of the 19th century could sometimes be run on a shoe-string and terrorism was considered at that time as a weapon of the poor. The modern terrorist groups, particularly trans-national groups, are quite affluent and funds needed to finance modern terrorist operations are substantial. Some of these groups have offices in luxury hotels, bank accounts in Switzerland and have an abundance of funds to make it possible for them to engage in kinds of costly operations beyond the reach of poorer terrorists. At the same time a surfeit of money also breeds corruption. Funds obtained from sponsors or raised by criminal operations are often diverted for the personal consumption of the terrorists.

Today, a new link between drug and terror has come into existence. Many modern terrorist groups no longer rely on bank robberies and other forms of crime to collect money for their various activities. Alliance with the drug traffickers gives them access to enormous funds which can be utilized against the target government. Thus money obtained from narcotics trafficking is utilized to support terrorism and the terrorists in their turn provide protection and assistance to the drug traffickers.

With technological advancement and miniaturization of weapons, a whole range of small, protable, but lethal weapons are coming into the possession of the terrorists. With technological advance, there is also a haunting fear that the terrorists may follow the ABC option-an acronym for "atomic, biological, chemical" weapons. Such ominous prospects cause a great deal of concern to security forces and contingency planners. In the UK, security forces have done considerable planning to fashion responses, particularly to the placing of improvised nuclear devices.There are also no unmanageable technological impediments to the capture of chemical and biological weapons by terrorists. It is often argued that most of the terrorist groups will not opt for the deadly option because that would defeat their purpose. Terrorists believe in tactical violence rather than in strategic, scorched-earth destruction. But some groups may opt for the weapons of super-violence because their aim will not be political change but total destruction of the enemy. Terrorist groups may not show the restraint that (whatever their atrocities) has characterized them in the past.

Terrorist groups function in small decentralized cells. Their infrastructure is centrifugal. This enhances their tactical flexibility and enables them to operate against the targets at their own convenience. This tactical flexibility is of great importance because of the asymmetrical power relationship between the terrorists and the government. Studies of terrorist groups have shown that there is no room for its members to entertain doubts. Very often, dissenters are eliminated with great ruthlessness and publicity. The problem before any terrorist organization is to reconcile the competing requirements of coordination of effort and security. In a planned terrorist operation certain individuals are strategically placed as 'sleepers' and activated as and when required during the struggle. Surprise is the corner-stone of all terrorist operations. As the security forces are stronger than the terrorists, the latter seek to minimize the disadvantage by choosing time, location and methods of attack. The membership of terrorist groups comprises different types of individuals with a variety of motives and motivations. In terrorist organizations there are crusaders imbued with a sense of idealism as well as 'crazies' and criminals. It is often seen that criminals and lumpen elements infiltrate into the ranks of the terrorists and perpetrate acts of unprovoked terror and violence to further their own personal ends.

Of course, one of the aims of the terrorists always is to provoke the authorities to use illegal, unconstitutional and repressive measures. If, in order to suppress the terrorists, the government uses draconian and extralegal methods and deprives the citizens of their human rights, it loses in the process both legitimacy and public support. It turns a "political situation into a military one", as Marighella has written in his *Mini Manual of the Urban Guerrilla*. And this is what the terrorists also want.

Today, the scourge of terrorism has become worldwide. It throws a complicated set of challenges varying in scope and scale to different state governments which often grope for appropriate means to respond. No fool-proof remedies against this difficult and persistent feature of international violence are yet on the horizon.

19
Role of the Army in Combating Terrorism

In a democratic state internal security duties are normally performed by the police, and the armed forces are viewed as an inappropriate agency for this purpose. But sometimes, to meet grave threats to internal security, the Army is called in to render assistance to the civil power. This is known as Military Aid to Civil Power (MACP).

Deployment of the armed forces to combat terrorism or insurgency has taken place in different countries at different times. Since 1969, a large number of British troops have been deployed in Ireland for containing the activities of the IRA and other terrorist groups. In 1970, the then Canadian Prime Minister, Pierre Trudeau, invoked the War Measures Act and deployed troops in the Montreal region to deal with the terrorism of the 'Front Liberation du Quebec' (FLQ), a group responsible for kidnapping the British Trade Commissioner, James Cross, and the Minister of Labour in the Quebec Provincial Government, Pierre Laporte. This Act remained in force for six months and gave sweeping powers of detention for questioning to the security forces.

In England in May 1980, a team from the British SAS (the Army's elite anti-terrorist unit) was deployed for launching an attack on the Iranian Embassy in London to effect the rescue of the hostage held there by terrorists. British troops also participated in a number of anti-terrorist exercises held at London's Heathrow Airport when the Palestinian terrorists were believed to be planning a SAM-7 missile attack on the Airport in January 1974. In India, the Army has been employed for counter-insurgency operations in Nagaland, Manipur, Mizoram and also for anti-terrorist operations in the Punjab following 'Operation Bluestar'.

Difference in the Role of the Army and the Police

In a democratic state, preservation of public order and containment of violence from the anti-social elements is the responsibility of the police. The police are to enlist public support and cooperation by combining firmness with restraint and using minimum force for controlling threatening situations. The ethos of the Army, however, is totally different. The Army is trained to use maximum force for speedy elimination of an enemy and need not be worried about loss of lives or damage to property, or for winning public support. So whenever the Army is deployed on internal security duties, a deliberate policy decision has to be carefully taken. Circumstances must warrant such a radical change in internal security duty operations. The Army comes into the picture when there is protracted violence beyond containment by the police. However, Army action invariably implies coercive action. Too often and too eager invocation of military aid to civil power may amount to repression. On the other hand, too great a concern for democratic rights and sensibilities may paralyse a government and ultimately bring about destruction of democracy itself. The problem is one of striking a proper balance. But if the Army is to operate successfully against the terrorists, it has to be adequately trained and prepared for such low-intensity, anti-terrorist operations. Intensive training is required for it. A highly trained military unit is an effective final back-up when normal police methods are insufficient.

In India, the use of the armed forces in aid to the civil power is provided for under Articles 130, 131 and 132 of the Code of Criminal Procedure. The Army or any other force which goes to the aid of the civil power remains under its 'control' and has to take orders from it. The civil power in the State is the State Government which functions through the cabinet in normal times and through the Governor during the President's rule. At district level, the civil power is represented by the District Magistrate. The concept of Martial Law is unknown in our legal system. It is the civil authority which retains full control and remains responsible for all the action, leaving to the commander of the armed forces discretion to utilize the forces under his command in the best possible way and to use such physical measures as and when necessary. The action at all stages should be preventive and not punitive or repressive and should end as soon as the objective is achieved. It is true that on many occasions the civil authorities try to help the Army to play its role properly by submitting to its demands and operational requirements. The clear legal position, however, is that the Army only assists and does not replace the civil authorities.

In any anti-terrorist operations where the Army has been deployed, it should be in close cooperation and coordination with civil authorities, police and paramilitary forces. Without the closest possible intelligence coordination contingency planning and tactical coordination between all the agencies, a successful drive against terrorists is not possible. In Malaya during the counter-insurgency operations, General Sir Richard Templar acted as Director of Operations under the civil administration to maintain the unity of command.

Third Force

It is argued that both politically and militarily the Army is not an appropriate instrument for dealing with internal disorder. For the government to use troops is to grant to the terrorist a kind of combatant status. The confrontation takes on a different nature and form. There is also the terrorist demand to be treated as political or military prisoners rather than as criminals, a demand which sections of internal and international opinion will be disposed to regard as legitimate. Once the military force is committed, it must in a physical sense be successful since the troops are the last resort open to the government and any major failure on their part would by psychologically disastrous for the government. It is argued that the commitment of troops should be pushed back further down the ladder of escalation. A Third Force, specially trained and equipped, would permit such a required type of graduated response. This graduation could be enhanced by the development of offensive and defensive operational equipment. The response would thus be limited, flexible and more amenable to political direction.

Many countries plagued by terrorist violence have set up units of thoroughly militarized police to deal with the problems. There are a number of existing models for such a force. The French have an anti-riot organization known as Compagnies Republicaines de Sécuritè (CRS) which is a highly mobile police security force under the control of the Ministry of Interior. The CRS is complemented by another mobile security force called Garde Mobile, which is under the Gendarmerice Nationale, a military force with mainly police duties. Although funded by the Minister of the Armed Forces, the Gendarmerie functions under the Minister of Interior when operating in aid to the civil power. If further assistance is needed, there is the national organization of Gendarmerice Nationale controlled by the Ministry of Defence. Its mobile groups can be brought into a support role anywhere in France and it has many special agencies. The force is equipped with machine guns, helicopters and scout cars, etc. Thus, the Army's loyalty and honour are not risked except in very special circumstances. However, in May 1968, disturbances in Paris demonstrated difficulties facing even so sophisticated a system. In West Germany, the Bundesgrenz Shutz (Federal Border Guard) is the unit to deal with acute internal crisis situations. Many other countries also have a Third Force, e.g., the Carabinieri in Italy and the Merechausse in the Netherlands. In India, new special Commando units have been set up by the government for countering terrorist operations. In the UK which does not have a Third Force, the Special Air Services (SAS) forms the Army's elite anti-terrorist unit which is on a constant three minute stand-by to go to the assistance of the police. There are also facilities for calling other specialist army units such as Army Bomb Disposal Teams. These army units have vital tactical mobility and range to counter terrorist attacks in different parts of Britain or in British waters.

Advantages

It is seen that these forces are specially trained to deal with particular situations like terrorist attacks and do not suffer from conflicting missions which is the case of both the Army (whose primary mission is to defend the country against external aggression) and the Police (whose primary mission is law enforcement and crime prevention). These specially trained units have operational skills to respond promptly to crisis situations. The use of a Third Force reduces the need to call in the Army who, with their training for war, may often use excessive force to deal with situations. Further, as far as possible, the Army should not be deployed for anti-terrorist operations which impinge on their training for war and dilute the deterrent impact of their deployment. The Third Force also removes the police from serious confrontation with members of the public and preserves their basically peace-keeping reputation.

However, some strong arguments against the proposal have been advanced. It is argued that specialized anti-terrorist training in the absence of experience of general police work may lead to the use of more force by the personnel than is necessary. There has been strong criticism of the Third Force in this regard, notably the CRS in France. In 1968, in Paris, the CRS was compared with the German SS. There is also the danger that the Government may use the Third Force to break up industrial protests or in situations that could exacerbate political tension and conflict. It is also argued that against the most serious forms of terrorist attacks such a force would not be militarily effective. Only the Army remains professionally competent to deal with such situations.

View in the UK

In Britain, the concept of a Third Force has been opposed on the grounds that ordinary members of the public would view with mistrust a fully militarized force and this would affect the present excellent police-public understanding and cooperation in Great Britain. In the United Kingdom the police are naturally unwilling to sacrifice the traditional role of a citizen in uniform. There is a feeling that the existence of a Third Force would be seen as a provocation and incitement to violence by the extremist. Memories of the Black and Tans would be roused and from many quarters cries of 'Gestapo' would be raised.

Restraint

When utilizing the Army against terrorists, it has to be seen that security forces act within the ambit of law. The response must be limited, well-defined and controlled. Any repressive over-reaction only plays into the hands of the terrorists and helps them to be seen as defenders of the people. The terrorists can also make propaganda capital out of such repressive measures. Adoption of a fortress mentality and decline of a State to a 'Permanent Sparta', forever watching extremist zealots, presents an image of society that the terrorist would impose if they were successful.

There are some sound reasons for limiting the internal security role of the armed services. The police operate in the midst of the community and thus get better information and intelligence to enable them to cope with threats to social disorder. This advantage is not available to the Army which normally does not function in the midst of the community.

Justice Hope in his 'Protective Security Review' has outlined the situations in which he considers use of armed force personnel to be quite appropriate. The situations are: (a) assault of buildings, aircraft and other forms of public transport seized and held by the terrorist with or without hostages. (b) cordoning off or protecting large areas where terrorists may seek to enter by means of violence (for example, an airport). (c) situations involving large or remote areas outside the police control such as the sea, or requiring special skills or equipment where police are unable to do what is required. But if the Army is to operate in such situations effectively, it has to be trained thoroughly. In Britain the specialist anti-terrorist role has been assigned to the SAS. In the rescue operation of the hostages from the Iranian Embassy in London, in May 1980, the SAS played its role with great efficiency and technical skill. It was also demonstrated that a highly trained military unit can be an effective final back-up when police methods are insufficient. By way of contrast the failure of the

United States rescue mission to Iran in April 1980, reveals the thin line between success and failure and underscores the absolute necessity for exemplary training, planning and execution for counter-terrorist operations.

An important step in any counter-terrorist strategy is to heighten public awareness of terrorist threats and the various measures necessary to combat it. It will, perhaps, be necessary to keep secret the details of operational contingency and many issues of counter-terrorist policy to allay public misgivings. Nevertheless, there is need for public education in the field. This point was emphasized by Mr. Robert Mark in his 1978 report on policing to the Australian Government. He emphasized that the general guidelines governing invocation of military aid to civil power should be widely publicized so that there is no misunderstanding of government's intentions or the respective roles, rights and duties of the Police and the Army.

20
Guns and Explosives

At present different criminal and terrorist groups are using guns and explosives with deadly effect to carry out their violent operations. The lethal weaponry has given them awesome destructive power. With the technological advance and miniaturisation of weapons, a whole range of small, portable and easy-to-operate weapons are coming into existence. This refinement of personal weapons is of great help to the terrorists. The weapons range from automatic guns to sophisticated explosives and triggering devices. These include MAC-II Revolver which can fire at the speed of 1200 rounds per minute and is completely silent, short-range anti-tank weapons and shoulder-fired rocket launchers.

During the last decade, a tremendous proliferation of these weapons has taken place all over the world and India is no exception. Crude bombs, hand-made guns and self-loading rifles have now given way to high-quality explosives, automatic assault guns, mines and other weapons of great lethality. The trend is illustrated by the qualitative difference in the nature of transistor bombing in Delhi in 1985, and the recent RDX bombing in Bombay.

The danger is aggravated by the fact that the States who sponsor terrorist groups for launching some kind of proxy war may not show any restraint in releasing some of the destructive or disposable weapons to the terrorists. This proliferation of sophisticated and portable weapons among the terrorists poses a very great threat. The quantum of weapons which included shoulder-fired surface-to-air stinger missiles supplied to the Afghan Mujahideen for a decade and half by the CIA was colossal. Automatic weapons like Kalashnikovs of Soviet and Chinese origin as well as the Pakistan version of M-24 were also supplied in thousands. The ISI (Inter Service Intelligence) of Pakistan which handled these operations diverted large part of this weaponry for its sinister operations elsewhere. Automatic rifles of lethal fire-power today are available in plenty in the hands of the terrorists in different parts of the world. In Jammu & Kashmir, over 8000 Kalashnikov assault rifles of different models and about 300 tons of explosives have been reportedly recovered from the militants since December, 1989.

RDX and SEETEX

It is observed that in traditional crimes, the criminals use low explosives. Occasionally high explosives meant for commercial use in coal mines, blasting operations, etc., are used for making bombs. The terrorist groups now have switched over to the use of high explosives for making improvised explosive devices—IEDs. Prior to 1985, Punjab terrorists used conventional simply designed bombs consisting of low explosives like black powder or incendiary materials which were activated by a safety fuse. But after 1985, there has been a marked improvement in the design of bombs—improvised explosive devices. Deadly Explosives such as C-4, SEMTEX, etc, are being used. In Bombay blast, about 300 kgs of RDX, popularly known as Research and Development Explosives (the commercial name being 'Cyclonite' or 'Hexogen Nitrate') is reported to have been used. The initiating device used in Bombay blast was pencil-timer which functioned like a chemical detonator. RDX was also successfully used in the blast that killed Rajiv Gandhi. In Rajiv Gandhi's assassination RDX was kept in a belt tied to a humanbeing on the waist and it was triggered by a battery-operated hand-switch.

SEMTEX is odourless and colourless, high explosive of choice for the terrorists all over the world. It's most famous target was Pan Am Flight 103, which exploded over Lockerbie in Scotland in December 1980, killing all 259 on board and 11 people on the ground. Scottish officials have held that a terrorist group called 'Popular Front for the Liberation of Palestine General Command' blew up the plane by concealing SEMTEX in a radio cassette player and smuggling it aboard in a suit-case. Semtex is also thought to have been used to destroy a French DC-10 over the Sahara last September, killing 170 people. The President of Czechoslovakia Vaclav Havel acknowledged that his Communist predecessors sold Libya alone 1000 tons of SEMTEX. According to him, this means that the world terrorism has enough SEMTEX to last for 150 years.

Plastic Explosive

A plastic explosive has a big advantage over conventional substances as it can be moulded into any shape and can be smuggled easily. It is difficult to detect plastic explosives which are currently available. X-rays do not reveal plastic clearly and such explosives are so stable chemically, until detonated, that they do not emit much vapor that can be detected. That is the reason why El Al, the Israeli Airline, does not rely on inspection devices before letting passengers board a plane. The El Al staff go to the extent of checking the contents of every suit-case laboriously by hand.

IRA Operations

IRA extremists in Britain have used bombs with deadly effect and precision. They blew up Lord Mountbatton in 1979 and nearly killed Prime Minister Margaret Thatcher in 1984 by blasting the hotel in Brighton where she was camping during the Conservative Party Conference. They also blew up Mr. lan Gow by taping a SEMTEX charge under his car. The car blew up when Mr. Gow switched on the ignition. In an international symposium on fire-arms and explosives held at ICPO-Interpol, Lyons from 1st to 3rd December, 1992, it was mentioned by the delegate from UK that from 1960 to 1992 about 3000 persons have been killed and 22,636 injured in 48,375 incidents of various violence in England and lreland. It is estimated that terrorists in Northern lreland have enough weapons to last for the next 10 years. They are in possession of SAM 7 Surface to Air Missile (International Views on Fire-arms and Explosives, CBI Bulletin, November, 1992).

USA

Easy availability of guns and weapons has significantly contributed to lawlessness in the USA. Accroding to latest figures published in the *Time Magazine (Time,* December 20, 1993), handguns owned in USA by citizens are 67 million and violent crimes committed annually with handguns are 6,40,000. An estimated total cost towards fire-arms injuries is 14 billion dollars. In USA gun laws are notoriously lax. Anyone above 18 can buy a fire-arm and anyone above 21 can buy a handgun from any shop. Only some States have prescribed a few days' gap between the date of order and the date of delivery. Manufacturers and dealers keep their records, but there is no obligation on their part to submit any return to any authority. Faced with escalating violence and murder by use of guns there is demand for strict gun laws in USA. FBI. Director Louis Freeh has proposed a complete ban on assault weapons. USA had 10,567 handgun murders in 1990 while there were just 22 in Britain and 10 in Australia. Strict control over guns in Australia and Britain explain this difference. Gun deaths have also gone down in Cananda after tight controls were put in force in 1978. The US Congress recently passed the Brady Bill mandating a five-day waiting period on handgun sales. Stricter gun control laws are anticipated, despite opposition from the powerful gun lobby spearheaded by the powerful National Rifle Association Group.

Britain forbids handguns to most people who are not members of gun clubs; members also must store their weapons at the club. According to Chris Nuttall, Director of Research and Statistics at the Home Office, only three robberies ended in death by shooting in England and Wales in 1990 and 1991, while more than 1700 died in the US. Just as surprisingly, there were only three times as many non-gun homicides in the US as in the UK, but 150 times more gun homicides. Nuttall denies the gun lobby's argument that it is people that kill and not guns. He argues that the very presence and availability of guns escalates the risk of wounding or death in every category of crime including fights in a pub or at home.

Japan

During recent years, Japan has been one of very few countries which has achieved notable success in reducing violent crime and one of the important methods used by Japan was strict control of the possession of fire-arms and even swords. In the Conference on Fire-arms and Explosives held at Interpol in September, 1992, the Japanese delegate reported that except law-enforcement and military officers, only 50 sportsmen have been permitted to possess handguns. During the year 1991, only 22 robberies with fire-arms have been reported in the entire country. Possession of fire-arms licence is considered as a privilege in Japan.

Smuggling of Arms from Pakistan

However, in some other countries like Pakistan gun control laws are believed to be very lax. A large number of authorities can even grant licences for possession of automatic weapons of Kalashnikov variety. In Pakistan the drug mafia, which holds a position of great influence, is also involved in clandestine arms trade across the border. It has been found by BSF authorities that from across the West Pakistan border three types of arms are smuggled into India—those made by Pakistan's ordnance factories, those made in countries other than Pakistan and Dera made. Dera is a bordering township in western Punjab where arms manufacture is like a cottage industry. These weapons coming in the hands of extremists and other subversive elements pose a grave security threat.

Arms and explosives have become sinews of crime and offensive terror in different parts of the world today. The present chaotic conditions in Russia and its adjoining States have led to loss-thefts of as yet unknown number of small weapons. According to one report, there is disappearance of nearly 25000 weapons from stocks. Again there are nearly 30 million weapons in the hands of different army formations in Russia, over which the control of the central authority is not adequate.

The recent figures given in the 'Crime in India-1991', prepared by the National Crime Records Bureau show that in India the total number of cases under the Arms Act in the year 1991 was 62,025 against the quinquennial average of 55,172. U.P. heads the list with 39,283 cases followed by Punjab with 2,738 and Rajasthan 2,453. The upswing in figures does not fully indicate the gravity of the situation. Clandestine manufacture and sale of illegal arms and their conversion and repair have also proliferated.

The crux of the problem is that in India at present too many people possess licences for holding arms. According to the figures made available by the Ministry of Home Affairs to the National Police Commission, there were 12,30,000 licensed fire-arms in 1964 and the number jumped to 14,12,000 in the year 1969—an increase of nearly 15 per cent in 5 years. The number has continued to increase since then. At present for any licensed fire-arm there are 3 or 4 unlicensed ones. It has been aptly pointed out by a veteran police officer that there are more fire-arms with individuals in Moradabad district of U.P. (about 22,000 licensed arms besides unlicensed ones) than in the whole of the United Kingdom or Japan.

In many dacoity-prone districts in India, particularly in Bihar and western U.P., the organised gangs of dacoits use weapons obtained from the licence-holders either by threatening them or making payments of money to them. Again, the bulk of ammunition used in country-made unlicensed weapons come from the licensed weapons as manufacture of ammunition is a complicated job which requires equipments not easily available. There is also leakage of arms and ammunition from army stores because of inadequate security arrangements and lack of accounting and supervision. A few years ago in a case of theft of cannon shells from an important army establishment, the officers of the Crime Branch of Orissa Police found during investigation that arrangements and procedures for accounting, storage and checking of arms and ammunition were far from being adequate and satisfactory.

Arms Act

It is absolutely necessary to take immediate steps to prevent proliferation of licensed and unlicensed weapons. The Indian Arms Act, 1959 was mild and did not provide strict penalties on illicit possession of arms. The National Police Commission gave a number of suggestions for the amendment of the Act of 1959. The new Arms Act of 1983 embodies some of the recommendations of the National Police Commission. The Act lays down enhanced punishment as well as minimum punishment for serious offences with the objective of providing necessary deterrence. But the mere amendment of the Act, though useful, will not be of help in containing the problem which has assumed alarming proportions. A number of other measures are called for to reduce drastically the number of arms licences. Law should be so amended that granting of licence for fire-arms should become a privilege. Only licensing authority should be the State Government, but the Government of India should fix a maximum number of licences for each State.

Even though the most common reason for owning a handgun is for household self-defence, studies suggest that loaded household handguns are more likely to kill family members than to save their lives. A Detroit study found that more people died in one year from handgun accidents alone than were killed by home-invading robbers or burglars in four and a half years (Newton and Zimring).*

The National Police Commission has further recommended that ordinarily a person should not be allowed to hold more than one fire-arm and he should not be permitted to purchase more than a limited quantity of ammunition. It shall be obligatory on him to maintain a very strict account of the ammunition purchased. Annual inspection of arms by both the licensing and police authorities must be done with greater care and vigilance. The present arrangement of inspection by police authorities often becomes an eye-wash. The National Police Commission has also suggested imposition of a condition that arms and ammunition should be kept in safe places to avoid their falling in the hands of unauthorised persons. Before issuing licence, it should be specifically ascertained if the licence holder is in a position to keep the arms in safe custody or not.

*ZIMRING, FRANKLINE. "Firearms and Federal Law: The Gun ControlAct of 1968," Journal of Legal Studies 4 (1975): 133-198.

21
Plea for a Magnimous View on Punjab Excesses

The alleged suicide of Ajit Singh Sandhu is deeply disturbing. His tragic end raises a few uncomfortable issues that call for a sober and balanced response. Sandhu, even his worst critics will admit, was a brave officer. In his emotion charged statement, K.P.S. Gill has mentioned that braving all risks and hazards Sandhu went to Tarn Taran as the Senior. Superintendent of Police to fight against terrorism when many of his colleagues, by various ingenious pleas, avoided posting in this terrorist ridden district. To them discretion was the better part of valour. He escaped death by a hair's breadth on a number of occasions, led his officers and men from the front and was responsible for the elimination of some dreaded terrorists like Gurbachan Singh Manochahal, Surjit Singh Bahla, etc., whose names had become bywords for terror and violence in Punjab. The tragic end of such a brave officer under inglorious circumstances calls for serious introspection and not an emotive reaction.

It is necessary to assess the measures taken by Sandhu and many other like-minded police officers against the blood-soaked backdrop of the reign of terror and violence that engulfed turbulent Punjab for more than a decade and sent shock-waves throughout the country. At one stage it almost threatened to tear apart the country's territorial integrity. It was indeed a violent secessionist movement aided and abetted by transnational forces determined to "do a Bangladesh" on India. During the period from 1981 to 1991, nearly 16,500 innocent people died in Punjab due to terrorist violence and this included more than 1,700 police officers and men. There was a clear game-plan behind the apparently indis-criminate and brutal killings by the terrorists. The plan was to bring about a mass exodus of the Hindus from the Punjab and to provoke a Hindu backlash against the Sikhs in other parts of the country resulting in the influx of more Sikhs to the Punjab. This would indeed make

Khalistan a reality. Fortunately, due to a variety of reasons and factors this did not come about. The age-old Hindu-Sikh amity in rural areas was able to withstand and frustrate this Machiavellian ploy. Pakistan's proxy war for India's balkanisation did not succeed.

Stamping out Terrorism

It is a known fact that one of the important reasons behind escalation of terrorism in Punjab in the eighties was the demoralisation of Punjab Police and the infiltration of extremists in its ranks. Sections of the Hindu populace even felt that Punjab Police was not non-partisan and clamoured for greater deployment of CRPF and BSF. In the revamping of Punjab Police and transforming it into an effective instrument for taking on the terrorists, capable police leaders like J.F. Ribiero and K.P.S. Gill played a very commendable role. It has to be always kept in mind that in any counter-insurgency operation, the role of the police backed by political leadership is of crucial importance. The army and the paramilitary forces cannot fill the role to be played by the police.

It was indeed the time for, to quote the words of Danton: "... audacity, more audacity and yet audacity" Many faint-hearted officers were leaving no stone unturned to avoid posting in Punjab. I personally know of some BSF officers posted in Punjab running from pillar to post to get their posting orders cancelled. I have knowledge of an officer of the Indian Audit and Accounts Service (IAAS) going to the High Court to obtain an injunction against his posting order in Punjab by offering various specious pleas. Other agencies of the government were also frozen and terror-struck into inaction. Almost a carte blanche was given to the police by the Central and State Government to carry on a war 'a outrance' against the terrorists armed to the teeth, flushed with funds and enjoying facility to withdraw, whenever necessary, to safe sanctuaries across the border. No questions were asked and no proper checks and control were exercised on police officers engaged in counter-terrorist operations. Some police leaders who wanted to exercise a moderating influence found themselves in a minority and quandary. The members of the public were also in favour of draconian measures. *Lex tailonis* was the rule. The cry of 'revanche' rent the air. In this connection it is important to bear in mind that abuses of authority by police can flourish not only because of official negligence or acquiescence but because, rightly or wrongly, broad sections of the people consider that in spite of their excesses the police are carrying out a necessary and unpleasant task if both State and society are to be preserved and protected. Such conditions create considerable moral burden on conscientious police leaders whose attitude and actions to check drift of this kind are of paramount significance.

It is an unfortunate fact that in the high noon of terrorism in Punjab there were many avoidable excesses by the police. They still rankle the hearts of many victims. Wounds have remained yet unhealed. The victims in many cases were innocent citizens and not the maniacal terrorists. In the National Human Rights Commission (NHRC) there are complaints of innocent people harassed and victimised because of their alleged links with the terrorists which on investigation have been found substantially correct. Sometimes even this fig-leaf of an excuse was not there. Often private scores were blantantly settled in the name of fighting against terrorism. Wrong means sullied the ends.

Branding Case

Further, police operations in dealing with the ordinary criminals and even common citizens got brutalised. The case of branding the foreheads of three female pickpockets with the word *Jebkatri* by a branding iron which came up before the NHRC is illustrative. In the case of *Inder Singh vs. State of Punjab and others,* the Supreme Court (1994 6 Supreme Court Cases 275) very adversely commented on abduction and possible liquidation of seven persons ranging in age from 85 to 14 by police officers using official machinery for the purpose. The court felt that the abduction was done on the suspicion of their possible linkage with terrorists. The court commented: "It was highly regrettable that a member of the police force should have resorted to retaliatory action and taken the law in his own hands". The court entrusted the investigation of the case to the CBI. One man refer in this connection to the perceptive observation of Prof. Twining *(Bentham on Torture)* that "institutionalisation of torture will lead to the creation of a guild of professional torturers and would open the door for a steady erosion of resistance to it in less extreme cases, until its regular use is accepted unthinkingly and ordinary people become conditioned to accept it as commonplace".

In counter-terrorist operations in different parts of the world it is noticed that one of the aims of the terrorists always is to provoke the authorities to illegal and repressive measures. It makes the security forces unpopular and "turns a military situation" as Marighella has written in his 'Mini Manual of the Urban Guerilla', "into a political one." The police and the security forces lose both legitimacy and public support.

Here it may be relevant to mention that the National Police Commission in its Fifth Report dealing with police encounters against the dacoits pointedly observed that "in spite of all practical difficulties we are convinced that this is not the remedy for this situation. The answer is to strengthen the law and the legal process."

Police Excesses

It is true that Punjab terrorism had been indeed one of the most lethal of all the terrorist campaigns in the world in the eighties. It was indeed a war-like situation. But even during a war there are humanitarian laws under the Geneva Convention (1949) forbidding torture, taking of hostages, outrages on personal dignity of prisoners of war and civilian population. Hence excesses against the alleged terrorist sympathisers, and at times against common citizens out of dubious motives cannot be by any means justified or condoned. It is very unfortunate that in that abnormal and extraordinary situation statutory agencies required to control and supervise police work had failed to do so. There was also political approval of ruthless police operations against the terrorists. Questionable methods adopted by the police were known and winked at. However, that can neither justify nor provide any legal excuse for the aberrations of the police commited during the period. The problem of untrammelled authority is that very soon it degenerates and becomes arbitrary in operation and random in effect. The police leadership in many instances failed to caution and exercise appropriate checks and control. The voice of sanity raised by a few was drowned in the cacophony of aggressive battle-cries.

Plea for Magnanimous View

Nowadays peace has returned to Punjab. One sees flickers of a new dawn after the long, dark and haunted night. Police officers who have committed wanton acts of violence and illegality are facing prosecution. It is time to consider if a more considerate and magnanimous view can be taken in favour of those who may have committed bona fide excesses in the discharge of their thankless duties. The acid test should be whether a person acted bona fide or not. Without showing clemency to those responsible for acts of illegality and cruelty against innocent and hapless citizens, it may be possible to take a more compassionate view in cases of others whose aberrations were bona fide and not motivated. The Truth and Reconciliation Commission in South Africa is thinking in terms of condoning the excesses of those who are making a clean breast before it of their omissions perpetrated during the apartheid regime Justice Shah, while enquiring into the excesses committed during the Emergency, adopted a similar reconciliatory approach in the case of officers for their bona fide excesses. Punjab's tryst with terror is perhaps over but it needs a strong police force, believing in human dignity and upholding human rights. Such a force enjoying popular support will be a stronger bulwark against the forces of terrorism and secession.

Section-V

22

Death Penalty for Rapists

The Union Home Minister, Mr L.K. Advani's proposal of death penalty for the rapists is more an expression of righteous indignation than careful and pragmatic response to a sinister problem assuming alarming dimensions. It is a fact that there has been a sharp increase in the incidence of this crime in different parts of the country. From the figures compiled by the National Crime Records Bureau, it is seen that 7,767 cases of rape were reported in the year 1989 and the figure shot up to 9,773 in 1995—an increase by 26 per cent. Indeed, the frequency of rape cases have now doubled during the decade 1985-1995—7,289 in 1985 to 13,754 in 1995 recording an increase of 88.7 per cent over 1985. In the year 1995, Madhya Pradesh, as in the previous years, recorded the highest number of incidents—3,119 which accounted for 22.7 per cent of the cases reported in the country. Further, statistics furnished in Crime in India—1995; prepared by the National Crime Records Bureau of the Ministry of Home Affairs also show that the conviction rate in rape cases during the year 1995 was barely 30 per cent.

Statutory Provisions

In this connection, it is important to bear in mind that crime statistics are notoriously misleading. On a very conservative estimate, 25 per cent of the cases are not registered; and due to the stigma and shame attached to the victim, rape remains one of the most misunderstood and unreported of crimes. A large number of cases of rape are suppressed and remain unregistered. Hence, increase in the incidence of the crime as reflected in the cases registered all over the country reflects the tip of the iceberg. The situation in this respect is not peculiar to India. The National Crime Victims Survey in Australia found that only 32 per cent of the victims of rape reported the assault. In a study of rape cases in the USA, Mr. S.C. Smithyman, "Characteristics of Undetected Rapists" found that for every 100 rape cases, only 25 are reported to the police, 13 persons are arrested and less than five are convicted. However, just making punishment for rape more severe will not act as a deterrent. Criminologists know that the real deterrent is the certainty and not the severity of punishment. Experience shows that passing of stringent anti-rape laws has not reduced the crimes. The Criminal Law Amendment Act, 1983, was passed as a response to the growing public opinion demanding more stringent anti-rape laws. It amends the Section 376 of the Indian Penal Code and enhances punishment of rape by providing that it shall not be less than seven years. If the sentence of punishment imposed is less than seven years, the court will have to mention in its judgement adequate and special reasons for this. It also provides enhanced punishment of a minimum of 10 years of imprisonment for police officers or staff of the jail or remand homes and other places of custody established by law. The Act amended the Code of Criminal Procedure and provided for trial in camera. It also inserted a new section in the IPC—Section 228(a) which makes the disclosure of identity of the victims in rape cases an offence punishable with imprisonment for two years. Unfortunately, passing of this fairly stringent anti-rape law has not reduced the volume of crime. Incidence of rape is sharply increasing in different parts of the country. Hence, it is wishful to think that the mere provision of death penalty for the perpetrators of the crime will serve as a deterrent. On the other hand, there is the likelihood that because of the enhanced punishment, the courts will examine and analyse the evidence more closely and refrain from imposing the maximum penalty because of the fear of miscarriage of justice.

Judicial Process

For a variety of reasons, a high percentage of rape cases is ending in acquittal in the court of law. Some of the reasons are shoddy investigation, negative medical opinion, inordinate delay in disposal of cases, thus allowing time to the accused persons to gain over the witnesses, etc. Investigation of rape cases requires extra-sympathetic handling of the traumatised victims. Investigators must establish proper rapport with the rape victims and help the latter to overcome the sense of shame, nervousness and reluctance. The victims feel embarrassed to answer delicate questions made by the investigating officers. Investigation of rape cases by female police officers proves very helpful. Unfortunately, the number of female police personnel in our country is totally inadequate. It is less than 2 per cent of the total force and female officers are available only in the big cities and in specialised wings of the criminal investigation departments. Female officers should also be trained in supportive and sympathetic interviewing techniques.

Negative opinion given by the medical doctors who examine the rape victims is another important factor behind failure of a large numbers of cases of rape in the courts of law. Sometimes lady doctors in government hospitals hesitate to give frank opinion for fear of appearing as prosecution witnesses and being subjected to embarrassing cross-examination. I personally know of a case in Sundargarh District of Orissa in which two officers of a well-known engineering firm were accused of rape of an *adivasi* woman by taking her out on the pretext of arranging a job for her. It was a true case which created a great commotion and *adivasi* workers of the factory went on a lightning strike. The case, however, ended in acquittal because in the medical report, the lady doctor gave an ambivalent opinion and also because of gaining over of some of the witnesses who impeached the character of the prosecutrix. The Law Commission in its Report (1980) has pointed out "the report of medical examination is often cursory and not sent in time". The Commission recommended some additions to the provision in Cr. P C, the most important being that "the report shall state precisely the reasons for which the conclusion is arrived at".

The courts also often impose lenient and not at all deterrent punishment. There is a well-known case where the court has exonerated two youngmen of the crime because that it felt that the accused suffered enough as undertrials. In many cases, maximum punishment is not imposed upon police officers in case of custodial rape by adducing some extenuating factors. Hence, the prime need is to speed up the trial of cases and impose deterrent punishment on the rapists.

There is very often an unfortunate delay in disposal of cases involving crime against women in the court of law. From a sample study of 100 cases of kidnapping and abduction done by the study group of the Bureau of Police Research and Development, it was found that the trial of rape cases prolongs for years, though Section 309 IPC provides for trial on a day-to-day basis. Prolongation of trial heightens the trauma of the victims. There should be all-out efforts to reduce the timeframe in disposal of cases in view of the agonising situations through which the victims and their family members pass through the trial stage. "Socially sensitised judge" in the memorable words of the Supreme Court,"is a better statutory answer against gender outrage than long clauses of complex sections with all the protection writ into it."

Bangladesh has now passed an Act (Act No.18 of 1995) for prevention of atrocities against women and children which provides that investigation as well as trial of rape cases should be completed within 90 days. Further, reports of the medical and forensic experts will be accepted as evidence by the courts without asking them to appear in the courts for tendering evidence.

Another problems of the rape victims at the time of trial deserves notice. Section 155(4) of the Indian Evidence Act, 1872 permits the cross-examiner to ask the victim of rape questions about her past character. These questions can be very embarrassing and place the victim under great emotional strain. It is necessary to amend the law in this respect and amendment of this provision has been recommended by the Law Commission of India in more than one of its reports.

Rape is a crime which has a devastating and shattering effect on the victim. For unmarried girls in our country, this ignominy destroys the chances of her ever getting married. Very often the victims do not lodge complaint and this failure to lodge a complaint is an indirect encouragement to the rapists. Fortunately, many women are now coming forward to report attacks on them. This has to be backed up by vigorous investigation and deterrent punishment of the malefactors. Mere enhancement of punishment will be a token populist gesture which will not help in the reduction of this crime.

23
Scourge of Child Prostitution

Child prostitution is one of the most cruel forms of exploitation of children. Children in prostitution are the pathetic victims of power and cruelty in a male-dominated society and greed-driven economy. Using children to satisfy an adult's sexual needs is so heinous and abhorrent that it does not exist even in the animal kingdom. The French jurist Renee Bridot said of prostituted children that "even if they are alive, they are dying within."

Today about 15 per cent of India's nearly 2 million prostitutes comprise children. Actually about 30 per cent of the prostitutes in the six major cities of India, viz. Calcutta, Mumbai, Delhi, Chennai, Bangalore and Hyderabad, as revealed in a report prepared by the Ministry of Human Resources Development, Government of India, (1994) were under 20 years of age and 39.4 per cent of the women entered the profession before they attained their eighteenth year. These figures are supported by evidence provided by the social workers who have first-hand knowledge of the red-light districts. They state that there are girls as young as nine years old in the cities' brothels. The survey also revealed that two-thirds of the prostitute population live below the poverty line and 60 per cent of them belonged to the Scheduled Castes and Scheduled Tribes and other backward classes. Very often various economic and cultural compulsions bear down on these infortunate girls and lead them to the slippery path of prostitution.

The Devadasis

In India, particularly in the remote and rural areas, religion and culture sometimes seek to sanctify and legitimise prostitution under the Devadasi system which exists especially in states like Andhra Pradesh, Maharashtra and Karnataka. The girls are initiated and transformed into Devadasis in ceremonies held in temples. A conservative estimate puts the number of prepubescent girls inducted in the system at 5,000 annually. These girls are forced to become Devadasis by a confluence of economic and social forces and are not just confined to religious ceremonial singing and dancing but take recourse to prostitution under the garb of Devadasi to subsist and feed themselves.

It has been observed that 95 per cent of the devadasis were born in Scheduled Caste families entrapped in poverty and illiteracy typical of these communities. These families largely depend upon the income provided by their Devadasi daughters. In a study on prostitution, Mrs. Joytsna Chatterjee mentions that a devadasi begins to work as prostitute only when she attains puberty. At that time the man who has paid for her dedication ceremony claims her as a concubine. In the state of Karnataka, to curb child prostitution, the Karnataka Devadasi (Dedication) Prevention Act, 1984 was introduced. However, it is necessary to take firm and energetic steps for proper implementation of the Act.

The Jogins

Similarly, the Jogin system which is endemic in Andhra Pradesh hinges on the manipulation of the Scheduled Castes by upper caste individuals. Jogins are condemned to a life of prostitution. A Jogin usually hands over her earnings to her family and meets her ends through manual labour. Apart from a life of prostitution, Jogins also have other duties such as dancing around corpses, and on certain festival days, etc. This form of rural prostitution brings the economic marginalisation of the Scheduled Castes and their exploitation by the upper castes to the fore.

The Bedias

The plight of the Bedia tribe shows how owing to acute economic distress prostitution can become the last resort of certain groups. About 2,993 Bedias women are estimated to be spread out in 16 districts of the state of Madhya Pradesh who are engaged in prostitution. Over the years, religious and social rituals were developed to legitimise prostitution into which girls are inducted when they attained puberty. Nowadays it is no longer a question of mere economic survival. A rigid scheme of things forces young women and girls to turn into prostitutes. Among the Bedias, it is not always poverty which forces the head of the family to engage his daughter in prostitution. Even rich Bedia men have been found to happily accept prostitution as additional sources of income. Of late, some NGO groups are intervening successfully to wean the girls away from their traditional profession through training and education.

It is seen that though child prostitution may have its lagistical origin in the rural areas, the end point for the child prostitute is urban brothels. Trafficking in women has now become an extremely lucrative operation. Bedia girls can today be found in most of the brothels of Indore, Delhi, Nagpur, Calcutta and Bombay.

Trafficking of Children from Nepal and Bangladesh

Trafficking in children has also become a trans-border operation. Nepal has become the largest identifiable source of child prostitutes in Indian brothels nowadays. A UNICEF review indicates that about 5,000 to 7,000 girls are brought into India from Nepal every year. Nepalese girls are highly in demand for their fair skin. A UNICEF survey further mentions that young Nepalese girls and virgins fetch at least Rs. 6,000 to 20,000 in Indian brothels on the first night. Further, virgins are prized because of the prevailing myth that sleeping with virgins will cure sexually transmitted diseases. Fear of AIDS also raises the demand for virgins.

Bombay has the highest concentration of Nepalese women in prostitution now. According to one estimate, there are about 20,000 women and girls from Nepal in the city's brothels. Many of the victims hailing from remote hilly villages and poor border communities of Nepal are lured by unscrupulous traffickers or neighbours with false promise of marriage or offers for employment. These hapless victims are then delivered to the brothel-owners in India. It is estimated that about 60 per cent of the girls may have contracted HIV infection.

According to a survey by, Bangladeshi girls and women constitute about 11 per cent of the total prostitutes in Calcutta. Difficult economic conditions in Bangladesh, and oppression and torture that many Bangladeshi girls suffer at the hands of their husbands, make Bangladesh a favourite operating ground for the traffickers. Most of the Bangladeshi girls in Calcutta brothels are from poor Muslim families tricked by the traffickers with offers of marriage or employment. Some of them are with children abandoned by their husbands. Faced with the desperate need to support and rear up the children, the girls have no other option except prostitution for survival.

City brothels do not provide 'dolche vita' to the prostitutes. More often than not they are cruelly and ruthlessly exploited. Prostitutes have to share almost 50 per cent of their income with brothel-keeper who, in his/her turn has to share it with the pimps, procurers, local dons and the police. Entrenched interests often act brutally and see that the young prostitutes do not get out their clutches or leave the profession voluntarily. Very often the girls are kept in a drugged or drunken stupor to quell resistance and pain that physically underdeveloped female bodies experience after sexual onslaughts. Further, internal injuries sustained from constant abuse place a child prostitute at a higher risk of contracting and then transmitting AIDS.

A study on child prostitution in West Bengal done by the National Commission for Women indicates that most of the child prostitutes drink alcohol at the behest of the customers and after a period of time it develops into a habit.

Sex Tourism

Another unsavoury fact to be kept in mind is that rapid growth of tourism in the decades 1970s and 1980s has coincided with the expansion of child sex industry in several countries. According to the World Tourism Organisation, tourism would be the largest industry by the year 2000. Tourist sex industries have proliferated in many countries of Asia. In Thailand, the sex industry is estimated to be worth over one billion pounds per year, servicing both Thai and foreign visitors. The number of sexually exploited children in that country is estimated to be more than 2 lakhs.

Unfortunately, India and other South Asian countries are replacing South-East Asia as the choice for the paedophile tourists as there are fewer laws against child sex abuse and South Asian children can be bought more cheaply. For example, in countries like Sri Lanka, the number of child prostitutes has increased dramatically with the growth of tourism in the island. PEACE, a non-governmental organisation working in the area, has estimated that about10,000 children aged from six to 14 years are virtually enslaved in brothels and a further 5,000 from aged 10 to 18 years are found in tourist resorts as sex workers.

A number of countries have enacted stiff laws to deal with the situation. New laws in the Philippines and Taiwan have also been enacted. Some foreign paedophiles are now on trial for child sex abuse in Thailand, Philippines and Sri Lanka. Many western countries have introduced an innovative 'law of extra-territoriality'. This means, in practice, that if one of their citizens sexually abuse a child in a foreign country or is party to sexual abuse, and is not tried for that crime in the country of the offence, he/she can be tried for the same crime in his/her own country. Germany introduced this law in 1993; France, Australia and the USA in 1994; Belgium and New Zealand in 1995. The result of the enforcement of these laws is not fully known.

Daughters: An Insurance Policy

Daughters of the prostitutes pose another serious problem. An active prostitute has frequent abortions and sometimes children. Barred from mainstream family life, prostitutes create their own family by refusing to abort at least one of their pregnancies. They try to raise their children with as much care and love as possible. This is proved by 32 per cent rise in the literacy rate of prostitutes between the generation studied by the Government of India and that of their children. Daughters of the prostitutes often suffer sexual abuse at the hands of the pimps or brothel-owners. The economic needs of the prostitute mothers often cause their daughters to enter the profession. As a last resort, the daughter is an insurance policy for aging prostitutes.

The Supreme Court in a Public Interest Litigation case, the *Gaurav Jain Petition*, observed that the children of the prostitutes should not be allowed to live in "an inferno and undesirable surroundings of prostitutes' homes". The court ruled in favour of shifting the children to the existing juvenile institutions. Unfortunately, most of these juvenile homes are in a bad shape, forcing children to flee these homes and return to their old surroundings.

It is also a fact that a large number of girl street children move from the pavements to brothels. Poor, abandoned and kidnapped children outside the pale of family protection are often exposed to abuse and rape. Later, they are forced into the flesh trade. One social activist, Maithli Shivaraman who studied cases of child rape among the working classes in Tamil Nadu observes: "Uncared for and unrehabilitated child victims form a source of recruitment to prostitution. The fact that minor prostitutes fetch a higher price than adults make vagrant children highly vulnerable and a prize-catch to the flesh trade."

Constitutional and Legal Aspect

It is a pity that, despite legal and constitutional bars, child prostitution has become a thriving business. Article 23 of the Constitution prohibits traffic in human beings. The Directive Principles of State Policy under Part IV of the Constitution in Article 39 (e) and (f) declare that childhood and youth are to be "protected against exploitation and against moral and material abandonment". India has ratified the Convention on the Rights of the Child on 11th December, 1992, and entered into the further obligation to ensure that the rights of children enshrined under it are protected throughout the country. Articles 34, 35 and 36 of the Convention impose serious responsibilities on the States to protect children from all forms of sexual exploitation and abuse.

Further, for dealing with the immoral trafficking in women, the Government of India enacted the Suppression of Immoral Traffic in Women and Grils Act, 1956. The Act was amended in 1986 and retitled Immoral Traffic (Prevention), Act 1956. The amended Act prohibits prostitution in its commercialised form without making it *per se* an offence. The Act prescribes stringent action against those inducting children below 16 years and minors between 16 to 18 years in the offence of procuring or taking a person for the purpose of sexual gratification. If the offence is committed against the child, the punishment is rigorous imprisonment for a term not less than 7 years which may even extend to life. The Act also provides for setting up "Protective Homes" for aged prostitutes who have been rescued from brothels.

The substantive law, i.e., the Indian Penal Code, also has several provisions which have bearing on certain conditions responsible for prostitution. Sections 366A and B provide punishment for procuring minor girls and import of girls from foreign countries. Section 372 provides punishment for selling and buying of minors for the purpose of prostitution. Sexual intercourse with a woman under 16 years of age, with or without her consent, under Section 375 amounts to rape and the offender is punishable with imprisonment for life.

Enforcement

Regrettably, the enforcement of the Act by the State Governments has been very poor. Often prostitutes and customers are arrested but further no thorough investigation into the criminal aspects of trafficking, violence and commercial exploitation of women and girls is undertaken. Consequently, the basic structure of this cruel and exploitative system remains intact. The various provisions of the Immoral Traffic Prevention Act are to be enforced through the local police set-up duly empowered under Section 13 of the Act. In vulnerable areas, the State Governments must appoint special police officers under Section 13 of ITPA. The special officers should be assisted by an advisory board comprising responsible local social workers of the area. This will create a mechanism at field level to grapple with the problem and take corrective strategies. Section 13 (4) of the Immoral Traffic Prevention Act empowers the Central Government to appoint "Trafficking Police Officers' with jurisdiction all over the country for investigation into the cases of inter-state trafficking in women. No step has so far been taken on by the Central Government in this regard."

In this connection it may be mentioned that alarmed by press reports regarding increase in child prostitution in the states of Tamil Nadu and Goa, the National Human Rights Commission issued notices to the two State Governments and the Department of Women and Child Development, Government of India, calling for reports on the prevailing situation. Both the Tamil Nadu and Goa Governments in their reports stated that there are no reported cases of child prostitution in their areas. This indicates that very often the State Governments are not facing the problem realistically and taking refuge behind official figures and statistics.

24
The Curse of Bonded Labour

In the National Human Rights Commission complaints are being regularly received regarding continuance of bonded labour in some areas of the country. It is an unfortunate fact that despite the enactment of the Bonded Labour System (Abolition) Act, 1976, the reprehensible bonded labour system in some form or the other prevails in different parts of the country. "We have yet to go a long way", said the Supreme Court in *Bhandu Mukti Morcha vs. Union of India,* "to wipe out this outrage against humanity."

A survey conducted by Gandhi Peace Foundation and National Labour Institute stated that there are about 26.7 lakh of bonded labourers in States surveyed by them. However, records of the Ministry of Labour indicate that only 22,000 bonded labourers were identified by the end of February, 1988. The identification of bonded labour is not even10 per cent of the conservative estimates of bonded labour in the country. Identification process is painfully slow. Necessary political will is lacking to come to grips with the problem.

International Instruments

Indeed the system of bonded labour is an outrageous violation of human rights. It is denounced in international instruments dealing with human rights. Article 4 of the Universal Declaration of Human Rights enjoins that: "No one shall be held in slavery or servitude". Again Article 8 of the International Convenant on Civil and Political Rights prohibits use of forced labour. In this connection, it may be mentioned that as far back as in 1930, long before the Universal Declaration of Human Rights came into being, the Forced Labcur Convention No. 29 was adopted by the International Labour Organisation (ILO). The ILO Convention defines 'forced labour' as all 'work or service which is expected from any person under the menace of penalty for which the said person has not offered himself voluntarily'. Article 2 of this Convention, however, lists some forms of forced or compulsory labour which are not banned or regulated by the Convention like compulsory military service, services exacted in case of emergency, services from a person as a consequence of conviction in a court of law. The Supreme Court in the case of *People's Union for Democratic Rights Vs. Union of India (1982)* held: "Exaction of labour and services against payment less than minimum wages amounts to forced labour and violates Article 23 of the Constitution."

The Bonded Labour System (Abolition) Act seeks to abolish the bonded labour system under which a debtor would render service to the creditor in consideration of an advance obtained from him. The Act by discharging the bonded labourer from an obligation to render any bonded labour breaks the nexus between the debtor and his labour. Provisions in Chapter III of the Act extinguish all the liabilities to pay the bonded debt. Section 13 of the Act also provides for the constitution of Vigilance Committees both at district and subdivisional levels for effective implementation of the Act. These Vigilance Committees have to perform duties of great importance. They have to identify bonded labour and take steps to free and rehabilitate them.

Unfortunately, this legislation which has been in force for two decades has not made any decisive impact either in the matter of identification, freeing and rehabilitation of bonded labour or in senitising people on the pernicious consequences of the system. The Chairman of the National Human Rights Commission, in a letter dated August 29, 1995, addressed to all the Chief Ministers mentioned that the International Labour Organesation (ILO) had taken note of the existence of bonded labour in certain sectors and expressed concern. The sectors referred by the ILO are stone quarries, migrant workers, *Jogins* and *Devdasis,* fishermen, *bidi* workers and carpet-weavers, etc. He urged the Chief Ministers of the concerned states to undertake a special survey in these occupations and take speedy and effective steps for the elimination of this outrageous system.

Indeed continuance of the bonded labour system is a major human rights problem in the country. An NGO group known as Anti-Slavery Society in a report to the UN Working Group on "Contemporary Forms of Slavery" at the Working Group's 1988 session mentioned that India has the largest number of bonded labourers in the world. The report highlighted the plight of the landless people of Bihar migrating to economically advanced regions like Punjab and Haryana and becoming agricultural workers bonded to creditor-employers or labour contractors. Indeed the passing of the Act has not relieved the age-old condition of debt bondage in the country.

In this connection it is worthwhile to mention the findings of the enquiry into the miserable conditions of the bonded quarry-mine workers of Faridabad done at the direction of the Supreme Court of India in 1983 by Mr L. Mishra, the then Director-General, Labour Welfare and Joint Secretary in the Ministry of Labour. The enquiry (the report has now been brought out in the form of a book *Burden of Bondage*) revealed how the bonded stone-quarry workers were subjected to long hours of work without any break and were engaged in a series of operations such as removal of overburden, drilling and blasting which involves use of explosives, cutting and breaking rocks to boulders and loading chips on the trucks. Born in condition of abject poverty and deprivation the workers were victims of indebtedness right from their birth. They were advanced some money by the agents of the contractors to liquidate loans of the money-lenders with the promise of higher earnings at the place of work to which they were lured. After that they 'enter a debt trap' and are unable to repay the loan because of the exorbitant rate of interest. Illiterate stone quarry-workers did not know the amount of advance taken by them at the time of migration and the amount repaid by them.

Unfortunately, bonded labourers also include a number of child labourers. According to an estimate projected by Human Rights Watch Group in their publication ("Small Hands of Slavery"), India now has about 15 million bonded child labourers. Bonded child labour is convenient, dependable, compliant and also replenishable. These children are sold to bond-masters. They work long hours over many years to pay off the debts because of the astronomical rate of interest and also the low wages.

It is seen that either due to lack of will or lack of support, Indian District Collectors have miserably failed to enforce the provisions of the Bonded Labour Abolition Act. In Tamil Nadu only in 1995 some employers of bonded child labour were arrested, kept in jail and fined nominal amounts. Actually labour laws and legal safeguards are regularly flouted. District officials of the Labour Department often collude with the offenders. A senior officer of the NHRC investigated into cases of bonded child labourers engaged in carpet weaving industry in Bhadohi in UP. The statements recorded by the police showed that they were brought from Bihar. Though information was given by an NGO group to the Labour Inspector (Enforcement) to conduct a raid at the premises of the factory owner, there was deliberate delay in organising the raid. Even when crimes have been detected, there were enormous delays in filling the cases before the court. Very often these Lobour Act cases are filed without providing age certificates of the children. Bogus names and wrong addresses of the employers are given. It is no wonder that the cases fail in the courts of law. Perhaps it may be necessary to insert a new provision under Chapter IV of the Act to impose a penalty on officers who knowingly or otherwise fail to enforce the provisions of the Act. The basic idea behind this provision should be to introduce an element of administrative accountability.

Indeed bonded labour system is like a hydra-headed monster which has to be attacked from many fronts. Enforcement of the law, though important, is not enough. The approach must be holistic. The bonded labourers must have some place to go. Without arrangement for proper rehabilitation, they will again fall back into bondage. This is happening repeatedly. In *Bandhu Mukti Morcha Case,* the Supreme Court issued directions to the Government of Haryana to adopt a scheme for more meaningful rehabilitation of the freed bonded labourers in the light of guidelines given by the Ministry of Labour, Government of India in its letter dated September 2, 1982 to various State Governments. The guidelines emphasised the need for psychological rehabilitation side by side with physical rehabilitation. Different components of rehabilitation should be integrated skilfully.

It may be mentioned here that a Study Group of the National Academy of Administration, in October 1989, highlighted some of the shortcomings in the implementation of the rehabilitation measures for the bonded labourers. These include time-lag between release and rehabilitation, non-integration of rehabilitation measures, problem of migrant bonded labourers and the lack of awareness among the bonded labourers about the various rehabilitation schemes.

Indeed it is a pity that determined steps have not been taken to end the bonded labour system. Continuance of this form of slavery is a blot on national honour. It exposes the country to international criticism. Further, it weakens our social fabric and saps its strength. Freedom that co-exists with servitude is illusory. In '*ASIAD workers' case,* the Supreme Court observed that the bonded labourers are "non-beings, exiles of civilisation, living a life worse than an animal for the animals are at least free to roam about as they like... ."

25
Child Marriage

Child marriage is an age-old social evil that has a long history. Various factors such as social, cultural and economic, are responsible for the growth of this baneful custom. In the past, it had its origin from the need to protect the unmarried girls from he covetous eyes of foreign invaders. Hence, early marriage of the children was preferred. Later on, it became a rigid social custom. The problem was further compounded by the dowry system. Fear of payment of heavy dowry for the marriage of a girl after puberty made the practice common, particularly among the poor and economically weaker sections of the society. In rural areas of some States, if the girl is not married before she has attained the age of 17 years, the entire family is ostracized.

It is aptly said that child marriage is an evil "more grave than Sati because it is far more devastating in its consequences and more insidious in its working". For the girl it leads to inadequate socialisation, discontinuation of education, great physiological and psychological damages due to repeated pregnancy. Child marriage increases the woman's reproductive span and shortens the inter-generation period. The Suicide Inquiry Committee, known as Hans Mehta Committee Report, pointed out that child marriage contributed to a large number of suicides amongst women in the then Saurashtra region. There is evidence to show that maximum maternal deaths take place between 15/16 years of age when a girl is no longer a child and yet unprepared for marriage. There is also evidence to show that more infant deaths take place when mothers are married below the age of 18 than when they are married at 21 and above. Literacy level of the mother and urbanisation are two important factors that influence the fertility rates, possibly because both lead to clearer awareness of the problems involved. Further, as has been seen in Rajasthan, not only the child marriage puts girls and their babies in the high risk categories, but also leads to high dropout rate from school for the young girls.

According to the Child Marriage Restraint Act (after its amendment in 1978), the minimum legal age of marriage in India is 18 years for women and 21 years for men. The Social Development Council, New

Delhi conducted a study of child marriages in Rajasthan and Andhra Pradesh and concluded that this piece of legislation to prevent child marriage remains a dead letter because of the prevalent social and religious customs, poor economic conditions, inadequate vocational employment and ineffective enforcement machinery. Although the prescribed age limit for the marriage of girls is 18 years, hundreds of girls are married in Rajasthan on the occasion *Aksha Tritya* as well as in some parts of Bihar, Andhra Pradesh and Tamil Nadu. The study conducted by the Council for Social Development for Ministry of Social Welfare, Government of India, has dealt with perception among women themselves on the issue of child marriage. Many women look upon early marriage as a protection against sexual molestation. Marriage of children at the time of death feast saves the expenses for another separate marriage feast. Again, when a girl grows up, it is difficult to find a suitable match. Dowry demand also goes up. Further, child marriage is actually a betrothal as 'gauna' or real marriage takes place when the girl is much older . Still, child marriage performed on *Aksha Teej, Fulera De* days are convenient as on these auspicious occasions the priests do not have to be consulted. Discussions with women also revealed the negative side of the issue. Boys who marry early have a tendency to abandon their wives and get remarried when they grow older. It is also seen that very often in Rajasthan the 'gauna' ceremony is hastened because of the parents desire to become grandparents as early as possible. According to a National Family Health Survey conducted in Rajasthan in 1993, 70 per cent of the marriages surveyed in the age group of 20 to 24 years were marriages before 18 years (a majority of women were unaware of the legal minimum age of marriage). In general 88 per cent of male children, and 87 per cent of female children were married before the legal minimum age. In fact, 1per cent of male children and 2 per cent of female children were married before the age of 10 years. The survey also noted that the mean age of daughters of mothers with high school education was 20. The corresponding mean age of marriage of the illiterate mothers was 15. The majority of the women (73 per cent) do not approve of child marriage.

Action by National Human Rights Commission

After publication of a news item in an English daily that child marriages will be solemnised on a big scale on 29th April, 1998, the day if *Akshay Tritya,* the National Human Rights Commission had issued a notice to the Chief Secretary of Rajasthan and called for a detailed report. It wanted to know of the action on the part of the administration in preventing child marriages. Senior officers of the Commission visited Bikaner and Jodhpur and witnessed that a number of child marriages were solemnised on that day with great celebration and without any restriction from the authorities or members of the public. The Commission had to point out to the State Government that it is a statutory obligation on its part under the Child Marriages Restraint Act to prevent child marriages and for taking appropriate proceedings in accordance with the provisions of the Act. It may be mentioned that earlier the National Human Rights Commission *suo motu* called for a report from the Government of Rajasthan on the prevalence of child marriage in the State. The government in its reply mentioned the measures it had taken to create social awareness against this longstanding evil. It stated that the Medical Health Department, Department of Women and Child Welfare have been organising meetings and seminars and publishing advertisements in newspapers, distributing handbills to sensitise people about the evil effects of child marriage and statutory provisions prohibiting the same.

The High Court of Rajasthan had earlier in a civil writ petition in the case of *Smt. Susheela Ghoshala vs. State of Rajasthan* expressed grave concern at the continuance of child marriages in spite of the Child Marriage Restraint Act, which is in force in the State. It pointed out that the child marriages are performed every year on a very large scale on the auspicious day of *Akshay Tritya.* This baneful custom has received tacit sanction from society and no social organisation has come forward to educate the masses about the undesirable consequences of the child marriage. The High Court in its judgement has also stated that apart from educating the people about the Child Marriage Act through seminars at village levels, the provisions of the Act should be made more stringent with deterrent punishment for the contraveners. Child Marriage Prevention Officers should be appointed under Section 13 of the Act to prevent marriages being performed in contravention of the provisions of the Act and for effective prosecution of the persons violating the Act. The High Court further suggested to the government to consider the feasibility of constituting District and Block Level Committees comprising social workers, and officers of the Revenue Departments who should hold regular seminars at village levels and educate the public about the undesirable consequences of child marriage. The government should utilise both electronic and print media to condemn the social evil.

It is necessary to make the legal provisions more effective. Section 12 of the Child Marriage Restraint Act confers powers on the courts to issue injunctions prohibiting child marriage, Sub-section (2) of Section 12, however, says that no injunction can be issued unless the court has issued notices to such persons affording him an opportunity to show cause against such injunction. As this procedure will consume time, marriages in contravention of the Act take place before the court passes order preventing marriage. Most of the marriages take place in the interior villages away from the seats of the courts. Therefore, the remedy provided by Section 12 is far from being effective. The punishment provided under

Section 3 (2)(6) of the Act is also inadequate. Section 3 prescribes simple imprisonment of six months or fine of Rs. 10,000 to Rs. 15,000 or both when a male above 18 years of age and below 21 years of age marries a child. Section 5 provides punishment of simple imprisonment which may extend to three months and a fine on a person who performs or conducts or directs any child marriage. It is absolutely necessary to enhance the punishment and make it more deterrent. There should be an obligation on every person present at the child marriage for objecting and advising the persons concerned or for reporting to the Child Marriage Prevention Officer. There should also be provision of imposition of punishment on every person who aids by presence or participates without objection or protest in the performance of child marriage. As the offence under the Act is not cognisable, no arrest can be made without an order of the Judicial Magistrate. This causes undue delay and fails to produce the desired deterrent effect. There should be powers given to Executive Magistrates and police officers for effective implementation of the Act.

The National Human Rights Commission carefully examined the provisions of the Child Marriage Restraint Act and felt that certain amendments of the Act are called for. The procedures for prosecution under the Act are cumbersome and the penalties are not deterrent enough. Further, public participation in the implementation of the Act was poor. The Commission felt that the Act has to be amended to make the offence cognizable, non-bailable and triable in a Sessions Court. However, there should be greater emphasis upon prevention of child marriages rather than bare annulment. Compulsory registration of marriages perhaps could act as an impediment to child marriages. The National Commission for Women also, it is learnt, had undertaken a study of the subject and suggested some amendments of the Child Marriage Restraint Act. It suggested that a new section, Section 6-A should be inserted in the Child Marriage Restraint Act of 1929, making the marriage of a minor viod when a minor is taken or enticed out of the keeping of her lawful guardian and is sold for the purpose of marriage and subsequently meant to go through such a form of marriage. In this connection it may be mentioned that economists who have applied the law of demand and supply and recommended that the reduction in the supply of women will enhance their status, should look at hard anthropological evidence which shows that the regions in India where sex ratio is extremely adverse like in Bihar, UP, Rajasthan, etc., are contrarily notorious for inhuman practices against women like polyandry, gang-rape and dowry murders, etc.

However, the basic fact is to be recognised that legal deterrents alone will not be able to control or eliminate the scourge of child marriage. Social conscience should be stirred against this evil practice. Enlightened voluntary groups should be encouraged to come forward to mobilise public opinion and create a climate of stern social disapproval of the traditional practice of child marriage.

26

Gender Bias in Police Investigation

The word 'investigation' has been defined in the Criminal Procedure Code as "all the proceedings under the Code for the collection of evidence conducted by a police officer or by any person (other than a Magistrate) who is authorised by a Magistrate in this behalf". In the case of *R. N. Rishbud vs. State of Delhi,* the Supreme Court has laid down the various stages of investigation as under:

(i) proceeding to the spot;
(ii) ascertainment of facts and the circumstances of the case;
(iii) discovery and arrest of the suspected offender;
(iv) collection of evidence related to the commission of the offence, which may consist of:
   (a) examination of various persons and reduction of their statements in writing, if the officer thinks fit;
   (b) the search of places of seizure of things considered necessary for investigation;
   (c) formation of the opinion as to whether on the materials collected, there is a case to place the accused before the magistrate for trial.

Under the Indian legal system, investigation has to be honest, fair and above board. For investigation is nothing but discovery of the truth and collection of material, for placement before the court. Section 154 of the Cr. PC provides that a copy of the FIR should be given to the informant free of cost. However, very often this is not done, and more so when women come to lodge the complaints to the police station.

I have seen during my long service in the police that very often complaints against women are not properly registered. Non-registration of cases is a malady afflicting the police administration throughout the country. On a conservative estimate, throughout the country, nearly 25 per cent of the cases are not registered and this is more so where offences against women are concerned. In an experiment carried out by a senior police officer in 1960s, the Deputy Superintendents of Police lodged imaginary FIRs at police stations incogniton. It was found that only 1/3rd of the cases were registered and the lowest registration was in respect of FIRs involving crimes against women. The position perhaps has not improved since then. A study done in Madras has shown that many cases of reported deaths by suicide by unmarried young women were actually cases of rape culminating in suicide and this fact came to light during post mortem examinations of the bodies of the victims. Further, under Section 160 of the Cr. PC women should not be required to visit the police station or any place other than the place in which she resides. Unfortunately, this instruction is not being followed in practice. Women who are reportedly involved or suspected to be involved in criminal cases are routinely called to police stations for interrogation and needlessly kept there for hours. Complaints of misbehaviour and sexual misconduct against them are often received.

Inviestigation of Crimes Against Women

In investigation of crimes against women, it has to be kept in mind that women victims require sympathetic handling. Investigators have to empathise with the tortured victims. Investigators dealing with crimes against women must respond sympathetically and imaginatively to the problem of the poor victims. If for investigation under the Prevention of Corruption Act, 1947, only special senior officers of the rank of the Superintendents of Police could be thought of, there is no reason as to why qualified investigators should not be earmarked for investigating into offences against women. Unfortunately, the number of women police personnel in our country is inadequate and they are available only in big cities and in the specialised wings of State CID. It is necessary to substantially increase the strength of women investigating officers in State Police forces and give them adequate powers for dealing with women victims of ghastly crimes.

The Supreme Court in the case of *Bhagwan Dass Vs. Commissioner of Delhi* (commonly known as Delhi bride burning case) recommended that a female police officer of sufficient rank and status in the police force should be associated in the investigation of such a case from its very inception. Unfortunately, this direction is honoured more in breach.

Today discrimination and disadvantage against women have become institutionalised. It has spread through the legal and political systems and perpetuated by lack of education and unemployment market. A survey done by the London Metropolitan Police shows that in UK women are very much unrepresented in the police and the judiciary. In the year 1990, the strength of the women in the Metropolitan Police Service of UK was 12 per cent of the total force. In India today, out of the strength of nearly 877,308 police personnel, the number of women personnel is just 7,706, almost less than one per cent. In the Indian Police Service in 1992, out of the strength of 2,805, the number of women officers was 54.

The number of women police personnel, unfortunately, is inadequate in our country and they are available only in big cities and in special wings of CID I recollect an incident of violence in Rajgangpur in Sundergarh district of Orissa, when, after commission of a dacoity, the womenfolk in the house were raped by the criminals. But during investigation of the case, the circle inspector suppressed the rape of women with a view to minimising the barbarity and seriousness of the offence. However, a lady sub-inspector from the CID who had come with the CID team found out the fate of the hapless women during interview and deliberate suppression of the crime by the police officers.

It is not only necessary to increase the strength of women investigating officers in State police, but also to train them in supportive and sympathetic interviewing techniques. In Australia increased use of female officers, and specially trained sex crime units, have produced positive results.

Sometimes courts also, on very technical and flimsy grounds, order acquittal in cases of offences against women where severe punishment would have had a deterrent effect. Even, as DIG, CID remember supervising a case in which a woman was brutally raped and murdered by some hoodlums in Cuttack district. The case was widely publicised and created a sensation. The Crime Branch after investigating the case submitted the charge sheet u/s 302 IPC. The Sessions Judge convicted all the accused persons, but subsequently on a technical ground, they were all later acquitted by the High Court.

Slow Disposal of Cases

There is also inordinate delay in disposal of cases involving crimes against women. From a sample study of 100 cases of rape, kidnapping and abduction done by a study group of Bureau of Police Research and Development it could be found that only in 34 per cent of the cases trials were completed in 6 months, 48 per cent of the cases from 6 to 12 months and in 17 per cent of the cases it took more than a year. The victims and their family members pass through great agony and anxiety at the trial stage and serious efforts should be made to reduce the time taken in the courts for the disposal of the cases. "A socially sensitised judge", in the memorable words or the Supreme Court, "is a better statutory answer against gender outrage than long clauses of complete sections of law with all the protection writ into it."

Bangladesh has now passed an Act which provides that investigation as well as trial of rape cases should be completed within 90 days. Further, reports of the forensic experts will be accepted as evidence by the courts without asking them to appear in the courts for tendering evidence. Perhaps, there is need for passing similar laws in our country.

Need for Repeal of Certain Clauses

Another problem of the rape victims at the time of trial also deserves notice. Section 155(4) of the Indian Evidence Act, permits the cross-examiner to ask the victims of rape questions about her past character. These questions can be very embarrassing and place the victims under great emotional strain. The questions may cover not only her association with the accused in the past but also her alleged immoral character. This can be checked only by amending the law. An amendment of this section has been recommended by the Law Commission of India in more than one of its reports.

However, another aspect of the problem has also to be kept in mind. The Criminal Law Amendment Act, 1983 which was passed by the Parliament as a response to public opinion outraged by reports of rape on women, provides enhanced punishment of maximum ten years' imprisonment for police officer or staff of jails or remand homes who take advantage of their position and commit rape on women in their custody. The Act further inserts a new section in the Indian Evidence Act. Section 114A, which lays down that in cases where the sexual intercourse by the accused has been proved, and the victim woman states before the court that she did not consent, the court will presume that there was absence of consent and onus will be on the accused to prove that the woman had consented to the act. The Supreme Court in the case *of Bhagwada Boghinbhai Horji Vs. State of Gujarat* (AIR 1983 Supreme Court,759) expressed the view that "instances of false allegations of sexual molestation which are made in western society by women who are gold-diggers and seek to extract money by holding out the gun of public disclosure are extremely rare in tradition-bound, non-permissive Indian society where by and large sex is taboo." Unfortunately, realities of the situation are sometimes different. Senior law enforcement officers can recount cases where women of easy virtue have been employed to level false allegations against police officers with a view to demoralising them. I know of a case in Rourkela where I was then posted as a range DIG in which allegations of gang-rape were made by a woman of easy virtue against a sub-inspector and three constables who had come to arrest her paramour. During enquiries the allegations were found to be false and engineered at the instance of elements trying to smear the local administration.

In order to command confidence of the public police investigation must have to be fair and free from any kind of bias of race, sex or language. This calls for emancipatory training for achieving attitudinal transformation and a new organisational culture. Senior law enforcement officers have a key role to play in effecting this transformation.

Section-VI

27
Indian Prisons

On appalling conditions in Indian prisons have many books and articles been written. Reports of the Mulla Committee (1980-83), All India Jail Manual Committee (1957-59) as well as the Annual Reports (1994-95, 1995-96) of the (NHRC) have highlighted the ills that bedevil the prison administration and advocated the need for both short-term improvements and long-term reforms. NHRC is trying to persuade the Central as well as State Governments to agree for a new All India Prisons Act whose draft it has prepared. The new act is to replace the old and outdated Prisons Act of 1894.

Statistics

Meanwhile, some quick and positive steps to improve the prison administration in the country are called for. In this connection it has to be borne in mind that the total number of prisoners in jails is small when viewed against the prisoners in many other countries of the world. The total number of prisoners in India, (as on 31.12.95) according to figures collected by the Bureau of Police Research and Development (BPRD) was 226158. The number of male prisoners was 219873 and female prisoners was 6285. Of this, the number of undertrial prisoners was 163092. This reduces the number of convicted prisoners to 63066. In a country of about one billion population the number of prisoners in jails, and particularly those undergoing imprisonment after conviction, is no doubt very small. Indeed prisoners work out to be .023 per cent of the total population of the country.

The situation in India in this respect is to be juxtaposed against what is prevailing in some of the developed countries of the world. In the USA today there are one and half million prisoners, and another three million are under penal control outside prison. Thus, nearly five per cent of adult males are under penal control. It is not, as a well-known penologist Nil Christe puts it, "crime control, but a kind of war situation". In Russia, there has been an exponentional increase in the prison population. In 1993, Russia had about 573 prisoners per 100000 of population and in 1995, it was 687 per 100000 population. In India there were about 23 prisoners per lakh of population in 1995. Prison population of China is also very high, but reliable statistics are not available. Today Russia and the United States are the two biggest incarcerators in the world. In Great Britain also prison population is going up. The present prison population in the UK is about 60,000. It is the product of a new policy of "get-tough-on-crime" and constitutes a departure from the old conservative British tradition represented by Winston Churchill who said that it was not decent to have so many poor people in prison.

In this connection it may be mentioned that academic research has shown little or no correlation between rates of crime and number of people in prisons. Increase in the incarceration are not necessarily followed by decline in crime. A study in the USA has shown that two States—North Dakota and South Dakota—each are virtually identical in terms of demographics and geography. South Dakota imprisons citizens at three times the rate of North Dakota but crime between the States is roughly the same for several decades (USA Department of Justice, Bureau of Justice Statistics, August 1995).

Undertrial Population

However, the disturbing aspect of Indian prison condition is the overwhelming number of undertrial prisoners. In many jails of the country they constitute more than 90 per cent of the prison population. Presence of the undertrials along with the convicted prisoners has many distressing consequences. It causes 'contamination of crime'. Many inexperienced young men coming in constant touch with the hardened criminals get coarsened and spoiled. It is a fact that many gangsters recruit members of their criminal gangs from these borderline, yet redeemable, offenders admitted to jails. Further, constant movement of undertrial prisoners goes to create serious problems for the prison administration. They are carriers not only of narcotics and other contraband articles but also of contagious diseases.

Wolf Report

In the United Kingdom, Lord Wolf in his report on 'Prison Disturbances' (April, 1991) observed that owing to overcrowding very often a substantial number of prisoners leave prisons more embittered and hostile to society than when they arrive. Lord Wolf proposed that for achieving humane and constructive prison regime, there should be a legal ceiling on the number of inmates in each prison which the Home Secretary should be able to extend only by obtaining parliamentary approval.

In the United States of America, the Supreme Court in two major decisions addressed itself to this problem of overcrowding. In the case of *Wolf Vs. Mcdonal, 1974,* involving pre-trial detainees, the court held that the principle of one man, one cell cannot be read in the 'Due Process Clause" of the Fifth Amendment. It held that the practice of putting two detainees in a cell meant for one person was not unconstitutional. In the case of *Rhodes Vs. Chapman,* the court went on to conclude that the "Constitution does not mandate comfortable prisons". Howeve, if overcrowding is not constitutionally impermissible, it no doubt tells on the health of the prisoners and affects the hygienic conditions. In the Indian context, it is absolutely essential to take serious note of this problem.

At present, in Tihar jail, there are about 9,000 prisoners against the capacity of 2,500. In Meerut Jail, it was found during a visit of NHRC officers that against authorised capacity of 650 prisoners, were are about 3,000 prisoners. 80 per cent of them were undertrials. Overcrowded prisons do not have space, facility and resources to provide prisoners their normal work, training and other educational opportunities. It has a knock-on effect on other aspects of the prison administration.

The All India Jail Manual Committee (1957-59) strongly recommended that there should be separate institutions for accommodating undertrial prisoners with adequate security and segregation facilities at each place where a central of district prison is located: This is necessary to relieve pressure on district prisons and work out suitable arrangements for dealing with the undertrial prisoners. The institution should be located near the court premises to reduce the problem and hazards of transporting the prisoners.

Transportation Problem

Indeed, the problem of transporting the prisoners from prisons to courts and back is a recurring one. There are many complaints before the NHRC from prisoners from different jails stating that they are not produced before the court on the dates of hearing because of non-availability of the police escorts. There was a harrowing case from Bihar where a prisoner could not be produced before the court for a year because of non-availability of police escort. The police, on the other hand, take the plea that it has no separate staff earmarked for escort duty of prisoners, and so they find it difficult to spare police for escort duties especially when law and order problems erupt. Provision of separate staff for escorting the prisoners to courts and hospitals has to be considered seriously. The Supreme Court in the case of *Rama Murti Vs. State of Karnataka* has suggested that escorting of prisoners should be done not by the police but by the prison staff and necessary steps should be taken for the purpose. It is necessary to quickly implement this recommendation.

Medical Facilities

Indian jails have very poor medical facilities. The Mulla Committee in its report highlighted woeful lack of facilities for treatment of the prisoners in jails. Disturbed by the rising incidence of deaths in police and jail custody, the NHRC had issued instruction that reports of deaths in police and jail custody should be sent to it within 24 hours. During the year 1995-96, 308 cases of death and in 1996-97, 700 cases of death in jail custody were reported to the Commission. One of the reasons for the high incidence of death in jail custody is due to utter inadequacy of treatment facilities in jails. Indeed society has an obligation, as the Supreme Court has mentioned in *Rama Murti's Case,* towards prisoners health for two reasons. First, prisoners do not enjoy access to the medical expertise that free citizens have and secondly, because of conditions of incarceration inmates are exposed to more health hazards than ordinary citizens. Prisoners, therefore, suffer from a double handicap.

For lessening the hardship of the undertrials, recently, the Supreme Court in a path-breaking decision in *Common Cause Vs. Union of India and others* has held that right to speedy trial is a part and parcel of right to life guaranteed by Article 21 of the Constitution. The court ordered release on bail of the accused person whose trial was pending for one year or more attracting imprisonment up to 7 years and who has already spent six months to one year in jail. Cases which are pending for more than a year but legal punishment is below a year's imprisonment could be closed and the accused acquitted with court's orders. The court said that it will not allow criminal prosecution in the country to operate as 'engines of oppression'. It was hoped that this memorable judgement of the Supreme Court will usher in a new dawn for thousands of undertrial prisoners, but unfortunately the situation has not improved significantly for a variety of reasons even after this judgement of the court. It is necessary for the court to appoint a committee to review the operation and impact of its judgement in reducing the number of undertrials in jails.

There is another handicap suffered by the undertrials. Section 62 (5) of the Representation of Peoples Act provides that "no person shall vote in any election if he is confined in any prison, whether under sentence of imprisonment, transportation or otherwise". The law, thus, bars all undertrial prisoners who cannot arrange bail including those charged for minor offences from the right to exercise of their franchise. The Supreme Court, however, has upheld validity of Section 62 (5) of the Representation of People Act 1951. The court held that the classification of persons in and out of prison is a reasonable one. In view of restriction on the movement of prisoner, he cannot claim that he should be provided facilities to go and vote. In the judgement of the restriction applies to all persons in lawful custody of the police which includes a prisoner detained during the investigation before a chargesheet is submitted against him. On the other hand, a person convcted and sentenced to imprisonment but released on bail was permitted to vote. The court justified permitting a person in preventive detention to vote by postal ballot, while denying the same right to undertrials in detention by holding that preventive detention is to prevent breach of law, while imprisonment on conviction or during investigation is subsequent to commission of crime and, therefore the classification is reasonable. The court has justified the restriction on the ground that criminalisation of politics is negation of democracy.

Improving Prison Management

For improving prison management the idea of privatisation of prisons is being debated and discussed by the penologists. At present in the UK, there are two prisons managed by the private sector. Six new prisons are being built and these will also be run by the private sector. This has become necessary because the prison systin has reached the maximum capacity of 60,000 inmates. In the USA too a number of states are givin some correctional services and programmes to private firms. Indeed some areas of prison management can be considered for privatisation for better care and treatment of the prisoners. Certain areas of prison management can be privatised on an experimental basis by contracting out particular services to private sector such as catering, medical care, maintenance of buildings, etc. Such participation of private sector in prison management will tone up prison administration and allow prison officers adequate time to concentrate on correctional programmes, security and other administrative matters.

28
Prisons and Human Rights

Prisons constitute a critical area of human rights concern. A person in custody in any civilised society cannot be reduced to the status of non-person, because he is in prison. Hence prison system must offer conditions that are compatible with human dignity and conducive to social mainstreaming. Article 10 of the International Covenant on Civil and Political Rights (ICCPR) mandates that - "All persons deprived of liberty shall be treated with humanity and with respect for the inherent dignity of the person". It also stresses that - "the reform and social readaption of prisoners" should be an 'essential aim' of the imprisonment. United Nations Standard Minimum Rules for Protection of Prisoners (known as "Standard Minimum Rules") adopted by the UN Social and Economic Counsel in 1957 provided guidelines for treatment of prisoners and reaffirmed the tenet that prisoners do retain their fundamental rights even while in custody.

The Supreme Court of India also in the case of Prem Shankar Shukla *versus* Delhi Administration (WP No. 1079 of 1979) and Sunil Batra *versus* Delhi Administration (WP No. 1099 of 1979) reaffirmed the principle that persons in custody should be treated with respect for the inherent dignity of the human being. "The goal of imprisonment", to borrow the words of Justice Krishna Iyer, is 'not only punitive, but restorative to make an offender, a non-offender'.

Unfortunately, human rights of persons languishing in prisons are often disregarded and violated. Most of the prisoners in are poor and crimes committed by them are not dangerous. However the option chosen by the society is to lock them up. There are thus contradictions and dysfunctionalities at the heart of the prison system. It is aptly said that the prison is a place where the ills of society are distorted and exacerbated.

In India most of the prisons are overcrowded and suffer from appalling mismanagement and lack of adequate medical facilities. Justice

Leila Seth Commission of Enquiry looked into the circumstances and sequence of events leading to the death of Rajan Pillai in Tihar Jail. In the report the committee referred to overcrowding, appalling sanitary conditions and shortage of medical staff in the largest prison of the country. It found that in the jail hospital, there were only six doctors to look after 9,000 prisoners and called it nothing but a 'token of medical facilities'.

Prison Population

In India the prison population is relatively small (approximately 2,40,000 prisoners). The present population works out to be 0.23 per cent of the total population of the country. The situation in India in this respect is to be yuxtaposed against what is prevailing in some of the developed countries. A report by the Bureau of Statistics of the US Department of Justice shows that as on 31st December 1998 there were 1.5 million prisoners in different prisons in the USA. This gives USA a national incarceration rate of 628 prisoners per 100,000 of population against India's 23 prisoners per 100.000 population.

A striking feature of the US Prison System writes Vivien Stern in her book "A Sin Against the Future Imprisonment in the World" is the intolerable racial disproportion. Only 6 per cent of the population in the United States is black (i.e. African-American) and male, but nearly 50 per cent of the prisoners in USA are African-American. African-American men are imprisoned nearly six times higher than white men.

Overcrowding

In India, however, 80 per cent of the prisoners are under trials and most of them stay in overcrowded prisons, where medical facilities are poor and inadequate. There are many jails, where prisoners are packed together with no space even to sleep. Indeed overcrowding remains a major problem in prisons of many other countries of the world. Panama's Modelo prison built in 1817, for example, held over 10 times the number of prisoners it was built to hold. The conditions were so notorious that, in a symbolic gesture the government finally demolished it on International Human Rights Day on 10 December, 1996. Many of the prisons in India and elsewhere are located in antiguated dilapidated nineteenth century buildings. There are nineteenth century prisons that lack functional system of plumbing. In Hong Kong, one of the technologically advanced cities in the world, prisoners in some older facilities have to "slop out" that is, to defecate in plastic buckets that were periodically allowed to be emptied.

Against this in some of the prisons in countries like—Columbia, India, Mexico, powerful jail inmates enjoy cellular phones, rich diets and comfortable lodgings.

Jail Deaths

One of the most common causes for deaths in prisons is disease. This often is the result of overcrowding, malnutrition and lack of medical care. The NHRC in India had issued instruction to all the State Governments to report within 24 hours all cases of deaths both in jail and police custody. During the year 1995-96, 308 cases, in 1996-97, 700 cases and in 1998-99, 1114 cases of death in jail custody were reported to the Commission. One of the major causes of death in jail custody in India is tuberculosis. This is also a problem in prisons of many other countries. A report of Human Rights Watch, a well known international NGO group, reveals that tuberculosis is the main killer in many of the Russian prisons. In Russia, the Prosecutor General announced in March 1997, that about 2000 inmates died of tuberculosis in that year. In Kazakistan also the disease has reached epidemic proportions in different jails.

In one case reported from Thane Central Jail, Maharashtra, (complaint petition of Jagannath Paoji Ingule), the National Human Rights Commission pointed out that "timely and proper medical diagnosis and treatment is inherent right of the prisoner. His freedom to seek and have access to medical aid outside is curtailed by law. Hence the prison authorities are therefore under duty to provide the reasonable degree of care and facility." The Commission in this case awarded an interim relief of Rs. one lakh to the dependents of the deceased prisoner and also directed the Maharashtra Government to make a comprehensive appraisal of the control and spread of tuberculosis and other infectious diseases in the prisons and to instal, wherever lacking, adequate diagnostic facilities.

Undertrials

For improving the prison conditions, it is essential to make determined efforts to reduce the number of under trials in jails. It was hoped that the Supreme Court's path-breaking decision in the case of "Common cause *versus* Union of India", in which the apex court prescribed different categories of cases pending trial where the accused prisoners can be released on bail. The court declared that it will not allow criminal prosecutions in the country to "operate as engine of oppression". Unfortunately, even after the judgement of the court, a large number of prisoners continue to languish in jails, because there is none to put up the cases on behalf of the prisoners before the courts. The judgement of the court was not self-executing. Again a large number of poor prisoners, though granted bail, continue to suffer imprisonment because there is none to provide sureties for them. In Tihar Jail at present there are more than 300 prisoners in this category.

Further the requirements of undertrial prisoners, who are yet to be found as guilty are quite different from those who have been convicted. From both administrative and therapeutic angles, separate institutions for undertrial prisoners would go a long way in rationalising and improving prison conditions.

Diet

One frequent complaint one hears from the prisoners is regarding the quality and quantity of food served to them. In the restricted condition of prison, the prisoners cannot get food of their choice or liking. Diet thus assumes special importance. Unfortunately, distribution of food, management of kitchen in most of the prisons are terribly unsatisfactory. The All India Jail Reforms Committee (1980-83) popularly known as Mulla Committee angrily remarked- "that in an era when careful attention is paid even to the feeding of the dairy cattle, prison kitchen and diet systems have remained in utter neglect".

Regarding violation of human rights in Indian prisons, the West Bengal Human Rights Commission in its annual report 1997-98 has highlighted some glaring cases. It mentions the case of an undertrial prisoner viz. Paresh Chandra Dutta, who was asked to pay by the jail staff Rs. 500/- for purchase of ten packets of cigarettes and bidis. On his non-compliance of this pre-emptory demand by the jail staff, he was severely assaulted by the Prisoner-incharge of the Ward. He was threatened that the assaults should continue till he made the required arrangement. The West Bengal Human Rights Commission found during investigation of the case that there was a custom in different jails to force undertrial prisoners to pay some money depending on his status and arrange give away like—cigarettes, bidis, etc. without which they would face serious trouble. Various other extortionary practices were also quite common in different jails and sub-jails. While recommending registration of criminal case against the sub-jailer and warders, who were on duty during the night of custodial violence on Paresh Chandra Dutta, the Commission awarded compensation to the wife of the deceased. It also asked the government to stop the ghastly convention inside the jail which caused untold sufferings to the hapless victims.

There was another case noted by the West Bengal Human Rights Commission in which a person was found detained in jail without trial for more than 14 years. The maximum sentence for the offence for which he was charged is 10 years' imprisonment. Noting the decline in the quality of 'supplies and services' in jail, the Commission suggested that the time has come when the Government may—"consider seriously to entrust some of the jail services to reputed NGOs, philanthropic bodies and organisations of ex-service men, etc. selectively".

Though the contradictions and aberrations in the present prison system are known, studies done in Western industrialised societies indicate that creation of more prisons for punishing the wrong doers is more popular than efforts at non-prison solutions. Retribution for those who have made others suffer is what the people want. Indeed concern for beter treatment of the victims of crime has given support to the idea that it is in the interest of the victims that the offender should be severely and adequately punished. Research studies however, show that victims of crime are perhaps less punitive than those who have not been victims. A study carried out in England of 300 burglary victims found that fewer than 30 per cent wanted the burglars to go to prison.

While it is necessary to look after the victims of crime, it will be perhaps worthwhile to remember that crime is not prevented by prison and the tendency to criminalise more acts is not helpful. While perpetrators of serious crimes and violence should of course be incarcerated, it has to be borne in mind that serious crimes constitute a minute proportion of the total crimes committed in a country. There is no need to think that locking up of a large number of persons in prison cells will make society more peaceful and violence-free.

An interesting study by Rand Foundation (Truth, Half Truth and Lies Myths and Realities about Crime and Punishment (1996) Marc Mauer and Malcolm c Young) shows that $2 million spent on providing cash and other incentives for disadvantaged young people to graduate from high school would result in a reduction of 258 crimes per year. If $1 million were spent on training for parents and family therapy for families with difficult children, 180 crimes a year would be prevented. The study estimates that if the $2 million were spent on prison, sixty crimes a year would be prevented. Vivien Stern has aptly said that indeed a time has come to think of shifting emphasis and resources of community from imprisonment to violence prevention, helping disturbed families, providing more educational opportunities and supporting children, who without such help will become the next generation of prisoners.

29
Privatising Prisons

The privatisation of prisons started in industrialized countries with Anglo-Saxon legal background and traditions like USA, United Kingdom, Canada, Australia in the mid 1970. In all these countries, there had been a sharp increase in prison population following the decision of the respective governments to getouhg on crime and lawlessness. For example, in the United States, the number of inmates in State and Federal prisons increased from 3,28,695 at the end of 1980 to 12,24,554 at the end of 1997. Authors Irwin andAustin described this trend as 'America's imprisonment binge'. There is also marked rise in the prison population in the United Kingdom. The present prison population in UK is about 60,000. It is a by-product of the new policy to 'get-tough on crime' and constitutes a departure from the old conservative British tradition represented by Winston Churchill who said that it was not decent to have so many poor people in prison.

The unprecedented growth of prison population resulted in serious prison overcrowding and a concomitant increase in correctional expenditure. These developments opened the doors for private corporations to finance and build prisons and also to operate and manage them. The promise of privatisation is that it can build, finance and manage correctional facilities cheaper and faster than the government agencies. Advocates of privatisation claim that private operators can run facilities more efficiently and cost-effectively.

Prison Privatisation in UK

In England, the Adam Smith Institute, the ultra-free market think-tank, in 1984 produced a pamphlet advocating privatisation of prisons. Initially it was viewed as an eccentric and unreliable idea not to be taken seriously. But in 1991 the law was changed to allow all types of prisons to be run by the private contractors. The race for privatisation was on. The first private prison in England called the Wolds catering for about

320 remand prisoners was opened in 1992 in North Humberside. This £ 30 million contract was won by the security company, Group 4. This was followed by setting up of prisons under private management at Backley Hall. Blakenhust in Hernford (run by UK Detention Services, a consortium of private companies) and Don Caster (run by Premier Prison Services).

Prison Privatisation in USA

In America, privatisation of prisons has proceeded at a feverish pace. In USA there are about 21 companies that manage 88 prisons which incarcerate about 50,000 inmates. This business has experienced a phenomenal rate of growth. Some of these private companies make hefty profits. The largest prison company, the Correction Corporation of America (CCA) had profits in 1993 of $ 4 million $ 100 million of revenue—a 57 per cent increase from the previous year. Founded in 1983, CCA controls 30 per cent of the private corrections market and is traded on the New York Stock Exchange.

Today, the United States has approximately 1.8 million people behind bars; about 1,00,000 in Federal custody, 6,00,000 in local jails and 1.1 million in State custody. Prisons hold persons convicted of federal or state crimes, jails hold people awaiting trial or serving short sentences. The United States now imprisons more people than any other country in the world—perhaps half a million more than Communist China. Mark Mauer, the author of the book *The Race to Incarcerate* says "No other society in human history has ever imprisoned so many of its own citizens for the purpose of crime control".

According to one estimate, if the present rate of growth of the prison population continues, 4.5 million black men will be in prison in USA by the year 2020. Nils Christie, a Norwegian criminologist, has argued in his book *Crime Control as Industry* that the massive prison expansion in the USA is one of the problems faced by modern societies. The problem is the emergence of a large group of unemployed young men whom society has no need of. He writes "It is a blessed situation for industry, but it is a fatal situation for the democratic ideals and for the basic values within our social systems". After USA, another country with real enthusiasm for privatisation is Australia where a larger number of prisons are being privatised than any other country. The State of Victoria has the highest number of private prisons than any other place in the world. In 1997, Victoria had 45 per cent of its prisoners in private prisons.

Debate

The debate between the opponents and proponents of privatisation surfaced early and continues unabated even today. In this debate the problems of justice and accountability feature prominently. The eminent criminologist Sir Leon Radzinowics said in 1988 when the issue of privatisation was first discussed in Great Britain "In a democracy grounded on the rule of law and public accountability, the enforcement of penal legislation which includes prisoners deprived of their liberty while awarding trial, should be the undiluted responsibility of the State". It is one thing for private companies to provide service for the prison system but is altogether a different matter for bodies whose motivation is primarily commercial to have coercive powers over the prisoners.

Advocates in favour of privatsation argue that private operators run facilities more efficiently and cost-effectively. Private prisons also provide more hours of purposeful activities for the prisoners. They further point out that the privatisation is the best way to decrease costs and construct new and better-designed prisons more quickly. By introducing an element of competition and new management techniques, cost can be reduced while ensuring improved quality of services. Private correetional services can operate more efficiently because of less bureaucratic 'red tape' and a higher motivation to control costs. Another valuable benefit of privatisation is that it introduces an element of competition in the field of corrections. Correctional officers and government agencies in the teeth of competition seek to improve theirr performance. The prison staff and their unions also behave more responsibly.

The greatest selling point in favour of private prison administration is that they are cheaper than state institutions. However, evidence on this score is somewhat inconclusive. A study done for the British Home Office by the accountants Cooper & Lybrand in 1996 shows that private prisons are by 13 to 22 per cent cheaper than public sector prisons. The study also shows that the cost gap is narrowing. In USA, the General Accounting Office of the Federal Government produced a report in 1996 based on an analysis of five studies that compared the cost and quality of private and public sector prisons. The report advised that no firm conclusion could be reached from the studies done so far. It could not be said categorically that private prisons are cheaper and better than public prisons.

American Federation of State, County and Municipal Employees while opposing contracting out of the correctional facilities poined out that staff salary and benefit levels make up approximately two-thirds of the cost of operating correctional facilities. Several major corporations involved in the privatisation of corrections have indicated that cutting salary and benefit levels is one way they plan to realise protits. In the attempt to cut costs, privatisation encourages investment in expensive electronic control to replace personnel. Private prisons are designed to minimise the number of staff required. In the long run, a decrease in human control will have negative consequences on the general atmosphere in prison.

Further, the critics also maintain that private companies may not take adequate interest in the rehabilitation of the offenders. Elements of rehabilitation may be incorporated in the contract, but are likely to be subordinated by profit motive in day-to-day practice. It has been found that in the Wolds prison in the United Kingdom prisoners are allowed 14 hours a day out of their cells but no activities are provided. At Borallon in Australia, the CCA tends to engage the inmates in relatively low-skilled and repetitive work rather than engaging in more expensive form of training so that they could undertake more skilled work. Another implication of privatisation is the importance of contract details and the monitoring of the private companies by the government personhel. Transition from rowing to steering is not always smooth. Performance of the private correctional facilities should be subjected to a vigorous external review by an independent authority.

In this connection, another development in USA requires notice. In USA, large-scale involvement of private companies in the construction and management of prisons has created what some people have called 'Prison Industrial Complex'. The analogy is with the military industrial complex. In the time of war, writes Vivien Stern, "it was more tanks and missiles and guns. In the age of prison industrial complex, it is more barbed wire prefabricated cells and electronic door-locking instruments". A whole sector of US industry is now devoted to war against the US citizens. The prison industrial complex, like the military industrial complex, is based on an 'iron triangle' between government bureaucracy, private industries and politicians. The three entities create inter-locking financial and political interests to push for a particular policy of expansion of the criminal justice system. It is this congruence of special interest that has given the prison construction in USA seemingly unstoppable momentum. Nils Christie in his *Crime Control as Industry* suggests that companies that service the criminal justice system need sufficient quantities of raw materials to guarantee long-term growh—the raw materials is prisoners and industry will do what is necessary to guarantee a steady supply.

Now, turning to the Indian scene one finds that conditions in Indian jails are appalling. There are serious problems of overcrowding, lack of sanitation, poor medical facilities and these deficiencies are compounded by utter mismanagement in the administration of jails. The National Human Rights Commission while suggesting various measures to improve conditions of the inmates in jails has recommended privatisation of some facilities like catering, escorting of prisoners from prisons to courts and prisons to hospitals and back. Similarly, the West Bengal Human Rights Commission in its Annual Report 1997-98 while noting the deeline in the quality of "supplies and services" in jails suggested that time has come when the Government may "seriously consider to entrust some of the jail services to reputed NGOs, philanthropic bodies and organisations of ex-servicemen etc. selectively". Response from the State governments so far has not been encouraging.

30

Indian Approach to Non-Discrimination Law

Discrimination means difference in treatment. The dictionary meaning of 'discriminate against' is to 'distinguish unfavourably from others'.

The Constitution of India guarantees equality and prohibits discrimination. The Preamble of the Indian Constitution expresses the solemn resolve of the people of India to secure to all Indian citizens "social, economic and political justice, liberty of thought, belief, faith and worship, equality of status, assuring the dignity of the individual". These noble ideas enshrined in the Preamble have been transformed into concrete legal propositions spread all over the Constitution. The first and foremost of these propositions are the Fundamental Rights and Directive Principles of State Policy. Most of the Fundamental Rights are available to all persons, citizens as well as non-citizens.

It may be mentioned in this connection that the Universal Declaration of Human Rights no doubt influenced the views and thinking of the framers of the Indian Constitution. The Universal Declaration of Human Rights was adopted by the United Nations General Assembly while debates in the Indian Constituent Assembly were going on. Hence it must be assumed, as the Supreme Court has said in the case of *Menaka Gandhi v. Union of India (A 1978 SC 597 para 70)* that the makers of the Indian Constitution in Framing Part III on the Fundamental Rights were influenced by the provisions of the Universal Declaration. It is, therefore, legitimate for the court to refer to the comparable provisions of the Universal Declaration in construing the intent and scope of the relevant text of Part III of the Constitution. The Supreme Court has also felt that not only the Fundamental Rights in Part III, but also the Directive Principles (Part IV) are based on human rights, so that the "Directives, even though non-justiciable, are not to be regarded as inferior to the Fundamental Rights."

Article 14 of the Constitution "prohibits State from denying to any person equality before the law or equal protection of the laws within the territory of India". Article 15 commands the State "not to discriminate against any citizens no grounds only of religion, race, caste, sex, place of birth or any one of them. On these grounds, on citizen can be subjected to any disability, liability, restriction or condition with regard to:

(a) access to shops, public restaurants, hotels and places of public entertainment; or
(b) the use of wells, tanks, bathing ghats, roads and places of public resort maintained wholly or partly out of State funds or dedicated to the use of the general public.

Notwithstanding these directions, the State is permitted to make special provision for women and for "advancement of any socially and educationally backward classes of citizens or for the Scheduled Castes and the Scheduled Tribes."

Article 16 ensures equality of opportunity for all citizens "in matters relating to employment or appointment to any officer under the State." It further enjoins that "No citizens on grounds only of religion, race, caste, sex, descent, place of birth will be ineligible for, or discriminated against in respect of employment or office under the State".

Article 17 forbids untouchability. Enforcement of any disability arising out of untouchability has been declared to be an offence punishable by law. Further, with a view to ensuring equality of status, Article 18 abolishes titles and prohibits their conferment by the State. Article 23 of the Constitution prohibits traffic in human beings and other similar forms of forced labour and makes the contravention of this provision an offence punishable by law.

Articles 25 to 28 guarantee freedom of religion. In the past, Hindu society used to exclude Scheduled Castes and degrade, condemn and humiliate them. Now this has been subjected to the laws "providing for social welfare and reform and throwing open Hindu religious institutions of public character to all classes and sections of the Hindus." Article 27 provides that "no person shall be compelled to pay any taxes, the proceeds of which are specifically appropriated in payment of expenses for the promotion or maintenance of any religion or religious denomination."

Article 29 guarantees every section of Indian citizens having a "distinct language, script or culture of its own, the right to conserve the same." It also prohibits denial of admission of any citizens into any educational institution maintained by the State or receiving aid out of State funds on grounds of religion, race, caste, language or any of them.

Scope of Articles 29-30

These two articles confer the following four distinct rights:

(i) Right of any section of citizens to conserve its own language, script or culture (Article 29 (1)).

(ii) Right of all religious or linguistic minorities to establish and administer educational institutions of their choice (Article 30 (1)).

(iii) Right of an educational institution not to be discriminated against in the matter of State aid on the ground that it is under management of a minorities (Article 30 (2)).

(iv) Right of a citizen not to be denied admission into State-maintained or State-aided educational institution on ground only of religion, race, caste or language (Article 29 (2)).

Distinction between Articles 15 (1) and 29 (2) of the Constitution has to be noticed. While Article 15 (1) is a protection against discrimination generally, Article 29 (2) offers protection against a particular species of wrong, namely the denial of admission into educational institutions maintained or aided by the State. While Article 15 (1) is available against the State, Article 29 (2) extends against the State or anybody who denies the right conferred by it. As pointed out earlier, the grounds of discrimination which are prohibited by the two provisions are not identical; 'language' is not mentioned in Article 15 (1) while 'place of birth' and 'sex' are not specified in Article 29 (2)..

It may be mentioned in this connection that the word 'minority' is not defined in the Constitution. According to the popular sense of the term, therefore, it should refer to any community which is numerically less than 50 per cent of the population of the State concerned, when the law which is impugned as violating Article 30 is a State law, applicable to territory of the State as a whole, and not any particular region thereof . Conversely, if it is a State law, a minority community of the State would be entitled to the protection of Article 30 (1) even though it may not constitute a minority in relation to the whole of India.

At various times, efforts have been made in international law to protect the rights of linguistic minorities. As a condition for membership, the League of Nations required some countries, newly established following World War I, to sign treaties guaranteeing respect for the rights of minorities, including their linguistic rights. In the post-World War II era, the main provision of international law dealing with this question is the International Covenant on Civil and Political Rights, to which 130 countries worldwide are state parties. Article 26 of ICCPR guarantees "equal and effective protection against discrimination" on various grounds, including language; and Article 27 asserts that: "In those States in which ethnic, religious or linguistic minorities exist, persons belonging to such minorities shall not be denied the right, in community with the other members of their group, to enjoy their own culture, to profess and practice their own religion, or to use their own language." Unfortunately, a number of countries that have legislated discrimination against linguistic minorities are among those that have ratified the covenant.

A number of European agreements also include provisions intended to protect the linguistic rights of minorities. The OSCE has been particularly effective, in large part because of its appointment of an unusually effective diplomat, Max van der Stoel, former Foreign Minister of the Netherlands, as its High Commissioner for Minorities.

The United States Supreme Court recently agreed to review a case in which the constitutionality of an 'English only' amendment to the Arizona Constitution was challenged. The American Supreme Court also in the case of *Mayer Vs. Nebraska* considered a Nebraska law that prohibited the teaching of foreign languages in public or private elementary schools. A teacher appealed against his conviction for teaching German in a parochial school. Justice James C McReynold in an important decision which is regarded as a classic of civil liberties jurisprudence, invalidated this attempt to spread xenophobia and also protected rights of the parents and their children's rights.

Article 32 gives a fundamental right to all citizens to move the Supreme Court for enforcement of these fundamental rights.

Directive Principles of State Policy

Part IV of the Constitution contains Directive Principles of State Policy. Directive Principles of State Policy, though not enforceable by any courts, are nevertheless fundamental in the governance of the country and it is the duty of the State to apply them in making laws. Among the Directive Principles, Article 38 provides that the "State shall strive to minimise inequalities in income and endeavour to eliminate inequalities in status, facilities and opportunities not only amongst individuals but amongst groups of people residing in different areas or engaged in different vocations."

Article 46 expressly enjoins the State to "promote with special care the educational and economic interest of the weaker sections of the people, in particular the Scheduled Castes and Scheduled Tribes and protect them from social injustice and all forms of exploitation". Articles

244 and 244A as well as the Fifth and Sixth Schedules of the Constitution make extensive provisions for the Scheduled Castes and Scheduled Tribes. It casts special responsibility on the Union Government to safeguard the interests of the Scheduled Tribes either directly or through the State Governments and allow maximum autonomy to the Scheduled Tribes in the administration of their personal and customary affairs and preservation of their culture and special identity. The makers of Indian Constitution had, thus, intense concern for the protection and advancement of Scheduled Castes and Scheduled Tribes and their equal participation and share in all walks of life. However, constitutional provisions are of little avail unless they are backed up by proper legislative and executive action. A number of laws have been enacted by Central and State Governments for enforcement of these constitutional rights.

In 1995, the Parliament enacted the Untouchability (Offence) Act which was renamed the Protection of Civil Rights Act, 1976. Civil rights under the amended Act is the right that accrued to the individual due to the abolition of untouchability. The Act makes all offences of untouchability non-compoundable and provides for summary trial for offences punishable up to 3 months, declares a civil servant showing negligence in investigation of offences as an abettor, brings privately owned places of worship within its purview, punishes preaching of untouchability and envisages an efficient machinery for the enforcement of the Act.

The Scheduled Castes and Scheduled Tribes (Prevention of Atrocities) Act, 1989, makes a very wide variety of atrocities committed against Scheduled Castes and Scheduled Tribes severely punishable. The public servants are under a positive obligation to enforce the Act and will have to face punishment for their failure to do so.

Executive Action

All affirmative programmes have to be implemented through proper executive action. Under amended Article 338 of the Constitution, a 5-Member Commission for Scheduled Castes and Scheduled Tribes known as the National Commission for Scheduled Castes and Scheduled Tribes was created. Article 164 of the Constitution provides that there shall be Ministers in charge of tribal welfare in the States of Madhya Pradesh, Bihar and Orissa who may in addition have charge of the welfare of Scheduled Castes and backwards or any other work. In some States, members of Scheduled Castes and Scheduled Tribes have held the posts of Chief Ministers and Governors and the current President of India also belongs to a Scheduled Caste.

Concept of Protective Discrimination

Article 16 (1) of the Indian Constitution itself permitted protective discrimination. The Supreme Court in the case of *State of Kerala vs. N.M. Thomas, AIR 1976 S.C. 490* dealt with the case in which the Kerala Government permitted a scheme showing favour to the Scheduled Castes and Tribes employees of the Registration Department by exempting them from passing the tests for promotion. This scheme was upheld by the Supreme Court as a valid protective discrimination under Article 16 (1) (Kerala is one of the States of the Indian Union).

In evolving a concept of protective discrimination, the Supreme Court judges were very much inspired by the values underlying the protection clause of the 14th Amendment of the American Constitution Referring apparently to *Brown vs. Board of Education and Civil Rights Act, 1964,* Justice Mathew agreed that "Beginning most notably with the Supreme Court's condemnation of school segregation in 1954, the United States has finally begun to correct the discrepancy between its ideals and its treatment of the black man. The first step, as reflected in the decisions of the courts and the civil rights laws of the congress, merely removed the legal and quasi-legal forms of racial discrimination. These actions while not producing true equality, or even equality of opportunity logically dictated the next step: positive use of government power to create the possibility of a real equality."

The court further observed any legitimate affirmative action rationally and reasonably administered is an aid to the attainment of equality In the words of Judge Tanaka of the International Court of Justice:

".... The principle is that what is equal is to be treated equally and what is different is to be treated differently, namely proportionately to the factual difference. This is what was indicated by Aristotle as *justitia commutativa* and *justitia distributiva.*

.... The principle of equality before the law does not mean the absolute equality, namely, equal treatment of men without regard to individual, concrete circumstances, but it means the relative equality namely the principle to treat equally what are equal and unequally what are unequal."

Compensatory Justice

Another judge of the Supreme Court, Justice Mr. Krishna Iyer, also felt that the problem of repairing the handicaps of the blacks in America was comparable to the problem of repairing the handicaps of the *Harijans* in India. Advancing the compensatory justice arguments, he remarked that since the society as a whole was responsible for the handicaps resulting from societal arrangements such as caste-structures and group suppressions, and these handicaps were relevant differences among men, compensatory treatment for the socially and historically disadvantaged groups was justified. Justice Mr. Krishna lyer referred to a case of *Schlesinger vs. Ballard.* In that case the American Supreme Court upheld a classification in favour of female naval officers by applying 'rational basis test'.

Case of Allen Bakke

Although unlike the Constitution of India, the US Constitution in specific terms does not authorise positive or protective discrimination, it was soon realized there that it was too hypocritical to talk about 'equality' based upon individual achievement when the deprivations and injustices were suffered by the Negroes as a group because of past and present societal discrimination. In the famous case of *Allan Bakke vs University of California,* the US Supreme Court gave a landmark decision on the constitutionality of benign racial preferences *98, SCR (US) 2733.*

In the *Allen Bakke's Case,* out of the 9 Justices constituting the Bench, four took a narrow statutory ground. They held that Allen Bakke was excluded only because of his race. This was impermissible. One of the Justices, Justice Powell decided Bakke's claim both on statutory and constitutional grounds. Justice Powell declared that racial and ethnic distinction of any sort is suspect and calls for exacting judicial scrutiny. He concluded "Nothing in the Constitution supports a notion that the individual may be asked to suffer impermissible burdens in order to enhance the societal standing of an ethnic group." The majority view affirmed the judgement of the California Supreme Court. It held that Allen Bakke was entitled to the admission because he was discriminated against on grounds of race and colour.

Four other judges, however, held the view that Davis' programme had not discriminated against the whites who had no history of past discrimination. These justices felt that both the 14th Amendment and the civil rights legislation mandated preferential treatment. Voluntary use of race for remedying the effects of past social discrimination was both constitutionally required and desired. The justices felt that to treat some person equally, he had to be treated unequally. This approach corresponded to the majority view in the case of Thomas.

Later on, in the case of *United Steelworks of America vs. Weber,* decided in July 1979, the US Supreme Court has by majority upheld a job quota for the blacks and has ruled that a company can use affirmative action programmes to remedy manifest racial imbalance in employment without fear of being challenged for its efforts in the court. Weber contrasts sharply with Bakke which explicitly disapproved quotas for minorities in admission to publicly supported universities. The Weber decision supports the conclusion reached by the majority in Thomas that 'equality' guarantee permits compensatory discrimination in favour of the disadvantaged.

In the case of *Indra Sawhney v. Union of India, 1992 Supp (3) SCC 217,* the Supreme Court dealt with the basic concept of reservation. The court stated "The fundamental question is what is the *raison d'etre* of reservation and what are its limits. The Constitution permits the State to adopt such affirmative action as it deems necessary to uplift the backward classes of citizens to levels of equality with the rest of our countrymen. The backward classes of citizens have in the past been denied access to government service on account of their inability to compete effectively in open selections on the basis of merits. It is, therefore, open to the government to reserve a certain number of seats in places of learning and public services in favour of Scheduled Castes and Scheduled Tribes and backward classes to the exclusion of all others, irrespective of merits."

The court also felt that: "Reservation is not an end in itself. It is a means to achieve equality. The policy of reservation adopted to achieve that end must, therefore, be consistent with the objective in view. Reservation must not outlast its constitutional object, and must not allow a vested interest to develop and perpetuate itself. There will be no need for reservation or preferential treatment once equality is achieved. Achievement and preservation of equality for all classes of people, irrespective of their birth, creed, faith or language is one of the noble ends to which the Constitution is dedicated. Every reservation founded on benign discrimination, and justifiably adopted to achieve the constitutional mandate of equality, must necessarily be a transient passage to that end. It is temporary in concept, limited in duration, conditional in application and specific in object. Reservation must contain within itself the seeds of its termination. Any attempt to perpetuate reservation and upset the constitutional mandate of equality is destructive of liberty and fraternity and all the basic values enshrined in the Constitution."

In formulating their approach to the question of non-discrimination the Indian courts have been very much influenced by international norms and conventions. The *Supreme Court* in the case of *Vishakha v. State of Rajasthan (Jt 1997 (7) S.C. 384)* held the view "in the absence of domestic law occupying the field, to formulate effective measures to check the evil of sexual harassment of working women at all workplaces, the contents of international conventions and norms are significant for the purpose of interpretation of the guarantee of gender equality, right to work with human dignity in Articles 14,15, 19 (1) (g) and 21 of the Constitution and the safeguards against sexual harassment implicit therein. Any international convention not inconsistent with the fundamental rights and in harmony with its spirit must be read into these provisions to enlarge the meaning and content thereof, to promote the object of the constitutional guarantee. This is implicit from Article 51 (c) and the enabling power of the Parliament to enact laws for implementing the international conventions and norms by virtue of Article 253 read with Entry 14 of the Union List in Seventh Schedule of the Constitution".

It is now an accepted rule of judicial construction that regard must be had to international conventions and norms for construing domestic law when there is no inconsistency between them and there is a void in the domestic law. The High Court of Australia in *Minister for Immigration and Ethnic Affairs v. Teoh, 128 ALR 353,* has recognised the concept of legitimate expectation of its observance in the absence of a contrary legislative provision, even in the absence of a Bill of Rights in the Constitution of Australia.

31
Forgotten Victims

In our present Criminal Justice System based on Anglo-Saxon adversarial pattern, the victim of crime who is the witness for the State against the offender is often forgotten and neglected.

During the last 100 years, there have been far-reaching changes in the Criminal Justice System concerning the rights of the accused during the investigation of crimes, prosecution of offenders and the punishment to be imposed in the event of conviction. Statistics on the offenders, details of arrests by the police, administration and release of the criminals from the penal institutions are all kept but collection of various aspects of information relating to the victims remains neglected.

It was only after the Second World War, that in the western countries like France, Germany, UK, as well as Canada, USA and Australia, there emerged a progressive school of thought in the Criminal Justice System which tried to shift the focus of attention to the victim who really deserves redress but often fails to get it. The historical evolution of the penal system from private vengeance to the state-administered justice has resulted in a Criminal Justice process in which the victims play only a secondary role. Scholars like Von Henting, Benjamin Mendelsohn and Henry Elenberger in their studies have all felt that in order to better understand the origin and implications of crime, it is necessary to study properly criminal-victim relationship.

A movement for the recognition of the victim of crime deserving a more effective remedy than the traditional practice of bringing civil suits was begun by English penal reformer Margery Fry in 1955. There was also demand for increased victim participation in the sentencing process. This was associated with studies which documented the victims alienation from the criminal justice system.

Studies of the victims before the law courts have revealed that their grievances are as much with the procedures of the Criminal Justice

System, particularly their lack of involvement in the decision-making process, as with the supposed injustice of the outcome.

Court Procedures

In the Anglo-saxon adversarial criminal justice pattern, the victim often finds the court procedures frustrating and cumbersome. The civil trial takes the form of the victim versus offender while the criminal trial takes the form of offender versus the state. The offence is not just against the victimised person but against the state. The state becomes the victim and not an arbiter in the struggle between the victim and the offender. If the victim feels that nobody cares for his suffering, it is in fact, so, because institutionally nobody does. Both victim and defendant have to stand as witnesses in the Court of Law during trial, but as the witness, the victim is more vulnerable than the defendant. The victim, unlike the defendant, can be asked about his history and character and he can be subjected to severe cross-examination by both the counsels. The status of the victim in the adversarial system thus remains quite vulnerable.

A very important grievance of the victims is their lack of 'standing' in the criminal processes. In the USA, a victim of crime while testifying before the Presidential Committee set up to study the condition of the victims said, "why didn't anyone consult me? I was the one who was kidnapped and not the State of Virginia." (President's Task Force and Victims of Crime 1982, p. 9). Research works on the subject done in various countries have shown that the victims demand not only compensation or punishment of the offenders, they also wish to be recognised as important and necessary participants in the criminal justice system. The 1990 report of the Compensation Tribunal in Victoria (Australia) documents that for the victims being heard is as important as being compensated.

The presumption that the prosecutor represents the victim is very often not correct. It is contradicted by the experience of many victims. If the public interest comes into conflict with that of the victim, the former prevails. Priority given to certain types of cases may determine the decision whether the offender will be prosecuted or not. Even when the offender is charged, there is no guarantee that the judiciary will be aware of the full impact of the crime upon the victim.

Prosecutors often do not disclose the details of impact of the crime on the victim to the sentencing authority. The extent of harm sustained by the victim is not revealed to the state authority, particularly in cases, where the accused pleads guilty or where there have been pretrial negotiations between the prosecution and the defence.

In America the new perception that criminal law should be responsive to the needs and problems of the victims was forcibly expressed by the President's Task Force on Crime, which asserted that, "Victims, no less than defendants, are entitled to their day in courts. Victims, no less than defendants are entitled to have their views considered. A judge cannot evaluate the seriousness of a defendant's conduct without knowing how the crime has burdened the victim. A judge cannot reach an informed determination of the danger posed by a defendant without hearing from the person he has victimised... (1982, pp. 76-77)".

The international community also felt the need to integrate the victim to the criminal justice process. The Seventh UN Congress at Milan adopted the Declaration specifically mentioning that the views and concerns of the victims are to be presented and considered at appropriate stages of the criminal justice process. The declaration was formally approved by the General Assembly of the United Nations in December, 1985.

Victim Impact Statements

Some sort of victims' integration in the criminal justice process has been tried in different countries. In the USA, and in parts of Canada, the right has been granted in the use of Victim Impact Statement (VIS). It is the statement made by the victim and addressed to the Judge. It contains descriptions of the harmful financial, social, psychological and physical consequences of the crime on the victim. The VIS in some jurisdictions, also includes the statement concerning the victim's feelings about the crime, the offenders and the proposed sentences.

In the US, plea-bargaining is one of the most common ways of disposing of cases. Many states in America have now passed laws that allow victim participation in plea-bargaining. In Australia, the National Committee on Violence has recently recommended that VIS should be introduced in all cases subject to some safeguards against abuse.

It has been argued in favour of the VIS that the effectiveness of the sentence will increase if the court is aware of the feelings of the victims. This will also result in increased victim cooperation with the criminal justice system, thereby enhancing its effectiveness. It has been sometimes argued that victims may turn out to be vindictive and the objective approach of the court may be influenced by the 'subjective pressure of the victim'. Research work done by the US Justice department shows that less than 10 per cent of the victims reported crime in order to see that the offender is punished. Very often the victim wants compensation, help and consultation rather than heavy punishment for the offenders even in cases where the offenders were strangers. A study conducted in Australia shows that the victims, particularly of serious crimes, expressed interest in receiving information concerning the case at all stages of the process.

Findings of Victimisation Surveys

Crime reviews are normally based on information collected by the police. It is a well-known fact that a large number of cases are not reported before the police and many reported cases are not registered. Like the criminologists, the victimologists were unaware of the true incidence of crime or victimisation.

The development of criminal victimisation survey has done much to change the situation. Victimisation survey has now created the second source of information. Victimisation surveys have been conducted in Great Britain, Australia, Canada, Netherlands and provided valuable wealth of information. It is now a regular feature of crime statistics in the United States.

In 1987, the proposal for an international victim survey was formally made at the Council of Europe conference. Up till now the survey has been carried out in more than 41 countries among more than 8,0000 respondents. The study was characterized by an authoritative reviewer as "a quantum leap in international statistics on crime and justice issues" (Lynch, 1993). **

In a paper presented at the 8th International Symposium on Victimology at Adelaide (August 21 to 26, 1994), the Director of European Institute of Crime Prevention and Control Mr. Matti Joutsen mentioned that the international victimisation survey revealed that in developing countries one of prime reasons for non-reporting of crimes was the negative attitude towards the police. The survey revealed that the few victims who turn to the criminal justice system run up against an almost total lack of victim services. Whereas victim advocates in developed countries are pushing for hotlines, shelters, special victim officers, baby-sitting services, transportation to and from the police station and the court, counselling and referral services to other agencies, such facilities are not just existing in developing countries. The reason cited by the governments is lack of funds. The lack of victim services aside, the victim often encounters insensitive treatment by the different criminal justice agencies from the police through to the courts.

In India, very limited efforts have been made so far of any kind of victimisation survey. The Institute of Criminology and Forensic Science

(ICFS), New Delhi, had undertaken two crime victim surveys. One with respect to homicide victims in Bangalore and Delhi, and the second with respect to those killed in motor vehicle accidents in Delhi. These two surveys yielded a rich harvest of data. They indicated that majority of the cases of homicides are single-assailant and single-victim phenomena, committed during evening hours by using sharp-edged weapons. The proportion of homicide victims belonging to Scheduled Castes and Scheduled Tribes is higher than their census proportion. Most of the victims were bread-winners for their families and belonged to lower and middle-income groups. In 88 per cent of homicides in Bangalore and 58 per cent in Delhi, victims and the offenders had prior interaction. The police have not been responsive to the emotional trauma of the victims, and the latter nurse a sense of grievance against the police. Further, a vast majority of the bereaved families were facing acute financial hardship after the death of their bread-winners. Not many individuals and volunteer organisations had come forward to help the distressed families.

The need of the time is to work out a coordinated policy to provide help and sustenance to the family members of the victims. Compensation to the victims of types of offence may not be pracatically feasible, but countries, had to be seriously thought of.

In an evaluation report on victim services in the US, Skogan* 'points to a mismatch between services and victim needs. Although the programme focused on counselling, many victims faced more mundane problems. When asked what help they needed that the programs could not deliver, more than half mentioned financial problems of frustration in arranging victim compensation. If this is the problem of the victims is an affluent country like US, the situation in a developing country like India can be well imagined.

Compensation

Provision of compensation to the crime victims is the crying need of the hour. International Covenant on Civil and Political Rights, 1966, indicates that an enforceable right to compensation is conceptually integral to human rights.

Article 9(5) of the Covenant reads as under:

> "Anyone who has been the victim of unlawful arrest or detention Shall have an enforceable right to compensation".

Switzerland had a scheme of compensation to victims of crime since 1937. In the United Kingdom, a Criminal Injuries Compensation Board within the Department of Justice of the Home Office started functioning since August, 1964; A crime compensation tribunal has started functioning in Newzealand under an Act of 1964 and in the United

States of America the States of California (1965), New York, (1967) Hawaii (1967), Navada (1969), New Jersey (1971), Alaska (1972), Georgia (1972), Rhode Island (1972) and Washington (1973) have introduced some schemes for compensation to the victims of crime and from the years shown against each.

It must, however, be stated that in the United States, the compensation to the victims of crime still comes more from the private insurance policies rather than from these schemes.

Victimology in India largely remains a non-starter. No comprehensive legislation, save in the fields of motor accident and factory injuries has yet been enacted. In India only provision regarding payment of compensation to the crime victim is contained in CRPC under section 357 which provides for compensation for loss or injury caused by the criminal offence to victim after fine is imposed by the court. The provision does not make it mandatory for the state to pay compensation to the victims. However, the amount of compensation has not been uniform and no cardinal principles have not been laid down. It is desirable to frame a suitable legislation under which the State should pay compensation to the victims of crime or to their kith and kin.

The Supreme Court, however, has stepped in the breach and interpreted the constitution for victimological justice.

While awarding interim compensation for wrongful detention, the Supreme Court in the [Rudul Sha Vs State of Bihar (Air 1983, SC 1086)] observed that "respect for rights of individuals is a bastion of democracy. Therefore, the state must repair the damage done by its officers to the petitioners rights". Taking into consideration the great harm done to the petitioner by the Government of Bihar, the Supreme Court ordered the State to pay to the petitioner a further sum of Rs. 30000/- as an interim measure in addition to the sum of Rs. 5000 already paid by it. The order of compensation was in the nature of a palliative and it did not preclude the petitioner from bringing a suit to recover appropriate damages from the state and its erring officials.

REFERENCES

1. Lynch James P. 'Understanding Crime: Experiences of Crime & Crime Control' (Rome, UNICR, pp. 175-89). The details regarding the survey has been taken from V. N. Rajan's article "Victimology in India" contained in the book of "Crime and Corrections in India".
2. Skogan Wesley G: "The fear of crime and its behavioral implications". Macmillan, pp. 167-88.

32
Controversy Around Capital Punishment

The Supreme Court's decision to uphold the death sentence of four persons convicted for taking part in the assassination of the former Prime Minister, Rajiv Gandhi, has sparked off the controversy over continuance of the death penalty in India. In the case of Rajiv Gandhi's assassination, the Special Court in Tamil Nadu convicted and sentenced to death 26 criminals. The Supreme Court while disposing of the appeal, commuted three of the death sentences to life sentences and released other 19 defendants on the grounds that they had already served seven years in judicial custody as undertrials. The Apex Court, however, upheld the death sentence against the remaining four: Nalini, Murugan, Santhan and Perarivalan.

In this connection it may be mentioned that the constitutionality of death penalty was last considered by the Supreme Court in Bachan Singh's case in 1980. The majority judgement then held it to be constitutional. The court did not accept the contention that capital punishment is violative of Article 19 of the Constitution because the freedoms guaranteed therein cannot be enjoyed without the basic right to live and that it defiled the dignity of the individual vouchsafed in the preamble of the Constitution. The court held that "in pith and substance, the penal laws do not deal with the subject matter of rights enshrined in the article and Section 302 of the Penal Code does not have to stand the test of Article 19". The court also did not buy the argument that the capital punishment did not serve any purpose and after surveying considerable literature on the subject concluded that the punishment might have some significant deterrent effect. It was also argued before the court that India being a party to the Stockholm Declaration of 1977 was committed to abolish capital punishment. The court after examining the relevant provisions of the International Covenant on Civil and

Political Rights which provided the basis of the Stockholm Declaration of 1977, held that the covenant did not stand for the abolition of death sentences but required that the penalty ought not be awarded arbitrarily and must be confined to extremely heinous crimes only. The court was satisfied that Indian position was identical to the covenant by virtue of Articles 20 and 21 of the Constitution and Article 354 (3) of the Criminal Procedure Code. The court cautioned the judges against being bloodthirsty and laid down that only in the "rarest of the rare" cases of exceptional depravity and brutality, death sentence should be awarded.

Today the trend in the world is towards abolition of death penalty. Fifty-seven countries including England, Germany, Italy and Brazil have abolished death penalty as a means to secure human rights. In Western Europe, death penalty is hardly ever applied. Belgium abolished it in 1996. Turkey retains the death penalty, but since 1984 has not carried it out. In San Marino, one of the Europe's smallest states, none has been executed since 1468.

Hanging

In India, hanging has been the well-accepted mode of inflicting capital punishment and the same has been provided in Section 354(5) of the Code of Criminal Procedure and in the Jail Manuals of different states. Constitutionality of Section 354(5) came up before the Supreme Court in *Dina* Vs *Union of India* {(1983) 4 SCC 645: 1983 SCC (Cri) 879}. The Apex Court did not accept the view that the mode of hanging is violative of Article 21 of the Constitution. The mode was invoked in many other countries of the world. The issue of public hanging came to the attention of the Supreme Court in *Attorney General* Vs *Lachma Devi*. This was a writ petition against order of the Rajasthan High Court regarding the execution of the petitioner by public hanging at a specified venue in Jaipur after giving widespread publicity. The Supreme Court held that public hanging, "even if permitted under the rules would violate Article 21 of the Constitution being barbaric, disgraceful and bringing shame on any civilised society".

Before the coming of democracy, South Africa was one of the world's greatest executioners. In 1987, there were more than three executions a week. However, the South African Constitutional Court in a recent ruling declared death penalty to be cruel, inhuman and degrading punishment and hence unconstitutional. The court concluded "poverty, race and chance play roles in the outcome of capital cases and in the final decision as to who should live and who should die".

China is regarded as the world's leading executioner. Amnesty International records 3500 executions in 1996 but assumed that the figure may be perhaps much higher. At least sixty-eight criminal offences, many of them non-violent, are punishable by death. These include killing a tiger, reselling VAT receipts, pimping, habitual theft or stealing cultural artefacts.

Opinion on the death penalty is being surveyed in the United States every year. In 1995, 77 per cent were in favour of the death penalty. United States leads the Western world in its enthusiasm for death penalty. The number of executions have grown steadily since the capital punishment was resumed in 1977. In 1995, there were 56 executions in the US against 38 in 1993.

Deterrent Effect

Death penalty is often justified on the ground that it will have deterrent effect on crime. However, such claims of deterrence are without any empirical support. Criminological studies have shown that capital punishment does not deter criminal behaviour. It precludes rehabilitation of human beings and is opposite of true atonement. Again, like all other forms of punishments, the error of judgement cannot be ruled out in the case of death penalty. Judicial error is always possible. In such cases, death penalty is an unpardonable crime committed against the society.

After examining all available information in 1968, the United Nation's Consultative Group on the Prevention of Crime and Treatment of Offenders summarized the situation in the following terms:

"Where it is used, capital punishment is increasingly a discretionary rather than a mandatory sanction. The Consultative Group also noted that a number of countries had abolished capital punishment for humanitarian reasons, irrespective of any possible deterrent effect it might be thought to have".

The UN Economic and Social Council in its resolution (resolution 1984/501 24th May 1984) laid down some safeguards for those facing capital punishment and one of the important safeguards is that persons below the age of 18 years at the time of the commission of the crime shall not be sentenced to death, nor shall the death sentence will be carried out on pregnant women, or on new mothers, or on persons who have become insane. Capital punishment may be imposed only when the guilt of the person charged is based upon clear and convincing evidence leaving no room for an alternative explanation of the facts.

International Standards of Human Rights call for abolition of death penalty or its use only in extremely limited cases. The United Nations Commission of Human Rights in April, 1999, passed a resolution calling on all states to establish a moratorium on execution with a view to completely abolishing death penalty. It also urged the states "to progressively restrict the number of offences for which the death penalty may be imposed".

In India, despite the ruling of the Apex Court, that death penalty may be imposed in the "rarest of the rare" cases, it extends to a wide range of offences. The Government of India in practice has applied the death penalty to a wide range of offences. Under the Indian Penal Code, death penalty can be applied for murder, gang robbery with murder, for abetting the suicide of a child or insane person, for waging war against the government, for abetting mutiny by a member of the armed forces, and for fabricating false evidence with intent to secure the conviction of other person for a capital offence when conviction ensues. Death sentences may also be imposed for a number of offences committed by members of the armed forces under the Army Act, 1950, the Air Force Act, 1950, and the Navy Act, 1956. In 1987, the Government of India passed the Commission of Sati (Prevention) Act, 1987, which applied the death penalty to individuals convicted of abetting a successful Sati.

It is well known in legal circles throughout the world that each court has some "hanging judges". Life and death of a person can, therefore, become a matter of chance depending on which bench of the court hears a particular case. This arbitrariness is unfair and against the rule of law. Today it is accepted in the civilised world that death penalty cannot be reconciled with human rights and liberal values. Further, death penalty effects not only the criminals but also his relatives and members of the family. They also get the marks of infamy. Studies made in different countries of the world have also found that percentage of poor persons being awarded death sentences is much higher than persons belonging to affluent groups.

The UN General Assembly on 15th December, 1988 adopted International Covenant on Civil and Political Rights: Second Optional Protocol, Aiming at Abolition of the Death Penalty. Article 1 of this Protocol provides that "no one under the jurisdiction of a State Party to the present Optional Protocol shall be executed", and that "each State Party shall take all necessary measures to abolish the death penalty within its jurisdiction". Article 5 of the Protocol provides for international monitoring of these provisions by the UN Human Rights Committee.

33
Police and Press in India—An Adversary Relationship

Law enforcement in a democratic society is a complex and complicated job. The work of the police as the main law enforcement agency is consequently a very difficult one because the police have to reconcile the dilemma of preserving liberty and human rights of the individual, on one hand, and enforcing laws which aim at the preservation of society from the operations of the anti-social elements, on the other. A policeman, it has been said, has to function in a democratic system, "as the battle-field for tension between the State and the individual," and hence conflict situations are inescapable in his work. The police officer, says Ben Whiteaker,[1] "acts as a lightning-conductor for resentment against many aberrations of society for which he is not responsible". Hence for successful performance of its multifarious responsibilities the police will have to depend on the willing co-operation and support of the public they serve. Any successful law-enforcement programme requires the backing of the informed and aroused citizenry.

The police can win communal consent and cooperation, if its image before the eyes of the public remains bright and untarnished. Webster, in his dictionary, defines image as the "mental representation of anything not actually present to the senses". The image of the police varies from country to cquntry. In some countries the police stand as the symbol of security and protection, while in some other countries the police are viewed as an object of terror, repression and hatred. The nineteenth century writer Alexander Herzen said that whereas seeing a policeman in Russia has an effect like a tile falling on one's head, in England the same sight increases one's sense of security.

Poor Police Image in India

In India for a variety of reasons, some of which are historical, the image of the police is poor and sullied. A study conducted in 1978 by the Indian Institute of Public Opinion, New Delhi, at the instance of the Ministry of Home Affairs, Government of India, and also a survey on the "Public Image of the Police" carried out by the Benaras Hindu University in 1972, revealed a very unattractive image of the police in the minds of the people. In these surveys an overwhelmingly large number of respondents described the police as inefficient, discourteous and partial towards the rich and influential.The surveys also interestingly revealed that those who had personal experience of some interaction with the police had a better impression of the police than those "who had formed their opinion on hearsay without any personal knowledge"[2]. A research study on the "Attitude of adolescents towards the police", done by the faculty members of the Institute of Criminology and Forensic Science, New Delhi, highlighted the fact that the attitude of the adolescent towards the police is very amenable to changes in the negative direction—"a word against the police is likely to be more effective than a word for the police".

Important Role of the Press

In this context the press has a significant part to play in shaping and moulding the attitude of the public towards the police. Though the image of any service or organization is ultimately based on the quality of service it renders, the important role of the press in brightening or smearing the police image cannot be overlooked. For improving communication and building bridges of understanding with the people, the police require the constant cooperation of the press. In this article the term "press" has been used to designate newspapers and periodicals and not electronic media like the radio and the television. In India at the end of 1977 there were 14,531 newspapers with a circulation of about 374.37 lakh copies. Though nearly 80 per cent of the people in the country are steeped in illiteracy, the educated citizens constituting the dominant and influential group and providing the leadership pool in a democratic society, are profoundly influenced by newspaper reports and comments. Many of them have a tendency credulously to accept anything which appears in print as gospel truth. They have neither the time nor the inclination for further verification. It is, therefore, absolutely necessary that police work, problems and constraints should be fairly and accurately projected before the public by the press. The Royal Commission on the Police (1962) stated in its report that the press and the broadcasting organization have a great influence in forming the popular image of the police, and this places "a great responsibility on the press to ensure that the police news and features are fair and accurate... It is most important that the press should maintain the highest standard in reporting police news. The public interest requires that people should have confidence in the police and any unfair or inaccurate reporting which undermines that confidence can do nothing but harm".[3] In the Indian context the role of the press is of greater importance because the electronic media being controlled by the government suffer to some extent from a lack of credibility.

Adversary Relationship between the Press and Police

Unfortunately, in our country a happy and harmonious press-police relationship has not so far grown up. More often than not there is confrontation instead of co-operation between the two. A content analysis of Indian papers and journals over a period of time will go to show the tendency of the press to make highly critical, negative and pejorative references to the work and conduct of the police. The press depict the police as insensitive, power-hungry and lawless. The police, on the other hand, accuse the press of sensationalism, exaggeration and distortion—all aimed at improving the circulation of the paper. Another police charge is that many press representatives are not only unsympathetic, but also betray a lack of understanding and objectivity while reporting crime and law and order problems. This adversary relationship between the police and press is unfortunate and undesirable. In a democratic system relationship between the police and the news media need not be always smooth, but despite occasional friction and "constructive tension", to use the phrase of a well-known journalist, there should be a large measure of understanding and a healthy appreciation of each other's role. On a more fundamental level, police officers have to bear in mind the principle that free and open news media fulfil an essential role in a democracy. They are the bulwarks of a free society. "Though the Athenian democracy modern State depends on its press, and so the freedom and quality of the press have become sure indications of the freedom and quality of a State. Nor has the situation greatly changed since the advent of the radio and television".[4]

Importance of Free Press

Moreover, the constitutions of democratic government have always sought to guarantee the freedom of the press. Article 19 of the Indian

Constitution guarantees freedom of speech and expression and the freedom of the press comes under the freedom of expression. The First Amendment of the United States Constitution has laid down that "the Congress shall make no law abridging the freedom of speech or of the press". The American statesman, Thomas Jefferson, in 1787, in a famous letter to Col. Edward Carrington, wrote "The basis of our government being the opinion of the people, the very first object should be to keep that right, and were it left to me to decide whether we should have a government without newspapers or newspapers without a government, I should not hesitate a moment to prefer the latter".[5]

Responsibility of the Free Press

A free press, however, must function with a sense of responsibility, impartiality and becoming restraint. "The true freedom of the press is to decide for itself", says Tom Wicker in his book *On Press*, "What to publish and when to publish it". In India the majority of the newspapers are in private hands—only 4 per cent of the newspapers are owned by Central and State Governments. A few big industrialists do control a chain of newspapers. The Press Commission had warned 15 years ago of this unfortunate trend and said that monopoly of thought was as bad as monopoly of wealth. This trend towards monopoly is also seen in the advanced Western countries owing to the dependence of the modern newspapers on advertising and the high cost of keeping pace with technical development. But where managements, however monopolistic, uphold the independence of their editors, the public service function of a newspaper can be served.

In our country, unfortunately, many newspapers which have sharp anti-government stance, often level their criticisms at the police when their real target is the Government. The present writer knows of a well circulated language daily which exaggerates every omission and commission of the police with a view to running down the ruling party in power. The present writer has also witnessed the problems and embarrassment caused to police officers in the field by unprincipled reporters of what may be called "muffasil papers". Reporters of many of these mushroom papers with questionable circulation figures, try to blackmail officers by threatening to print stories of a scandalous nature against them. This can be an irritating nuisance, but a self-respecting police officer should not submit to it.

No Character Assassination

In a democracy none can question the right of the press to try to serve the people by vigorously exposing abuses of authority, dereliction of duty and outright corruption of the police. Indeed the press has a watchdog role to play. Society and law-enforcement benefit where the press exposes these "cancerous pockets". But the press criticism should be based on facts and the object should be a constructive one of improving the functioning of the police and not running down the entire law-enforcement machinery. Maliciously slanderous and defamatory attacks on officers which tend to demoralise them should be avoided. Trammelled by the Government Servants' Conduct Rules, it is difficult for policemen to defend themselves and reply to allegations, even when a case is not sub-judice, without the sanction of the proper authority. For example, r. 22 of the Orissa Government Servants' Conduct Rules clearly lays down "No Government servant shall, except with the previous sanction of the Government, have recourse to any court or to the press for vindication of any official act which has become the subject matter of adverse criticism or an attack of defamatory character".

There is also some substance in the charge levelled by police officers against the press that untrue allegations are rarely corrected even when they are proved to be false. This tendency of the press not to admit inaccuracies except under pressure from the court is a bad symptom. The Press Council should prescribe a rule that whenever allegations against officers are made and reported a newspaper should be obliged to report the eventual determination of its outcome with the prominence.

Misconduct of the Police

Misdemeanours by policemen and stories of prosecution and conviction of police personnel are frequently given prominence in the press. It is a fact that the press is interested in "news". "The defaulting policeman", to quote the words of the Royal Commission, "like the defaulting person or school teacher is news".[6] The upshot is that the misconduct of some black sheep tends to tarnish the image of the entire service. Many people adopt the infamous "guilt by association technique of Senator McCarthy" and smear the police with the failings of one or two officers. "Though the duty of the press to report news accurately, even if it is unfavourable to the police, cannot be questioned, occasions do occur when the press does disservice to the police because the news is reported inaccurately or distorted, particularly in headlines".[7] There is also a reluctance on the part of senior police officers to frankly admit lapses and omissions on the part of their subordinates. Newsmen complain that senior officers even try to cover up or whitewash the lapses and try to defend the indefensible. Lord Devlin has said that "it is the general habit of the police not to admit the slightest departure from correctness". It is however, desirable that whatever serious lapses or acts of misdemeanour on the part of police personnel are reported, senior police officers should take an enlightened pre-emptive move and come out with a frank version and brief the press about it instead of trying to suppress it in a short-sighted manner. Failure to do so will prod the press to expose, and perhaps exaggerate, the misdeeds by gathering information from other sources.

Culture of Secrecy

This underscores the need for fostering a more candid, open-door and "fulfilling" police-press relationship based on mutual respect and understanding of each other's role and responsibilities. The complaints of the newspaper reporters against the police are that the police are unnecessarily secretive about divulging information to the press. Information, they allege, is usually withheld until it has lost its news-value. In analysing this charge of newsmen one can argue that at times it becomes difficult for the police to come forward with full details of any occurrence because the matter is "sub-judice", or, in the interest of the investigation of the case. Police investigation and subsequent judicial proceedings will be prejudiced if the press is told too much, Novertheless, there is also an undeniable tendency on the part of the police to withhold instead of sharing information with the press, either on the pretext of secrecy, or because no regular facility exists for it. In many police organizations there is adherence to a closed mouth and "no comment policy". Police Manuals of many States in India encourage a culture of secrecy and expressly prohibit police officials from making statements to the press. In several States the Superintendent of Police cannot hold a press conference and SHO is not permitted to provide any information to the press. Orissa Police Manual Rule 710 enjoins that "A police officer may not, unless specially empowered by the government, communicate to the press, any documents or information which have come into his possession in the course of his public duties or has been prepared or collected by him in the course of those duties, whether from official sources or otherwise".

The National Police Commission, after carefully examining the matter, has recommended[8] that every district Superintendent of Police should be permitted to deal directly with the press. The police stations should also be permitted to give statistical details of the number of crimes registered, arrests made, cases convicted, etc. The Commission has strongly advocated the sharing of as much information as possible with the press. "The exercise of discretion should be in favour of giving as much information as can be given". Often because of the failure of the police to communicate quickly to the press authentic facts regarding crime and disorder, the journalists rely on unverified information. Sometimes they even lend credence to rumours and send inaccurate reports and cause damage that no later denial, even if made, can ever repair.

Emphasising the same point, the Delhi Police Commission has said in its report[9] that, "the police case has often suffered because of its non-availability to the press", and has recommended that in respect of important happenings in which the police figure, relevant facts should be immediately given to the press in the form of handouts so that the press is in possession of all the meterial before publishing it. The Delhi Police Commission has further expressed in favour of a "code of honour" between the police and the press about what particular information should be published so that the "progress of investigation in any case is not jeopardised".

Unfortunately, police relations with the press generally remain limited to defensive contacts with a few crime reporters and releasing of occasional success stories to the press. Police officers have seldom taken initiatives, either to build up proper understanding with the newspaper editors and responsible columnists, or tried to explain to the public, through the press, police problems and various constraints that plague the police organization. Enlightened police officers should grasp the fact that the press in general is a potential ally and not a rival, and the more open and accountable the police are, the more likely they are to be supported and their problems and work appreciated. "But it is not just good enough" says the Royal Commission in its report," for the police to understand the requirements of the press. It is equally important that the press should understand the difficulties of the police because the interests of both, despite occasional friction, run in the same direction". "Mutual understanding", writes the journalist David Shaw," is clearly in the interests of both the police and the press and of the public that is ultimately served by both"

The press can also render service to the police and improve its image by disseminating information on departmental rules and giving publicity regarding wanted persons, criminals, etc. Regular news releases by the police on topics such as safe driving, general rules to be followed by members of the public at crime scenes, etc., will go to enhance its image before the public.

Crime Prevention Publicity

In the USA police forces in different States have tried to encourage the citizens to provide useful information to law-enforcement officials regarding unsolved crimes through a programme known as "Crime of the Week". Under this programme there is publication in papers and broadcasting on radio of the details of important unsolved crime; citizens are requested to provide information to the police about this particular case or about any other unsolved felony crime. Once the case is cleared the informants receive rewards. Under this programme police and media become allies in the battle against crime. A "solved crime of the week" translates into a success story for both the police and the media. It is a welcome contrast to the negative approach where criminals" "success stories" abound.[10]

An assessment of the crime prevention publicity done by the Research Unit of the Home Office, London,[11] shows that offender-orientated publicity campaigns through news media in the United Kingdom on vandalism, driving after drinking, careless driving, etc., intended to increase the fear of detection among the people by informing them of changes in legislation or law-enforcement practices, achieved some noteworthy success. The assessment report says, "From what has emerged so far, it would seem that one of the most useful roles publicity can play is in aiding the implementation of crime prevention measures involving new legislation and stiffer law-enforcement. It may help to justify the introduction of initially unpopular new measures through highlighting the social and personal costs of irresponsible behaviour".

The press can boost police morale and build up the police image by appreciating and supporting the work of sincere and conscientious law-enforcement officers who are discharging their duties braving many odds. The police job is a difficult one and can be unbelievably thankless and stress-filled. The hard core of honest and professionally motivated police officers require full public support and encouragement. "Let us give them respect", as the then President of the United States said[12] when addressing the graduation ceremony of FBI officers "respect that money cannot buy, but which they are trying to protect society from those who seek to endanger or destroy it".

Unwelcome Effect of Police-Baiting

The press should also remember that constant police-baiting and incapacity to appreciate the moral and professional problems of the policemen will have an unsettling impact on the morale of the police.

Psychologists have frequently demonstrated that self-regard is closely linked with perceived regard for one's self by others. Police morale will remain unsure and self-respect brittle if the public attitude towards the police influenced by the press remains constantly critical.

Again, opinion about the police cannot be separated from the feeling about the laws which they are required to enforce. Many of these laws are unenforceable. Actually, framers of laws give very little attention to the problems of enforcement and spend more time in debating the moral and abstract implications of such legislation. As a result, many of these laws, once enacted, are dumped like "unwanted babies at the backdoors of police stations with little or no inquiries as to their eventual health".[13] But public criticism against the ineffectiveness of the laws is directed at the police. The press can help the police by advising citizens to become more active politically and get such laws altered instead of resenting their enforcement by the police.

On a more fundamental plane, the press can be a useful ally of the police in the battle against crime and lawlessness by informing and educating the public that crime prevention and control will not be possible through police efforts alone. "People should now begin to ask as much of the courts, schools and prisons as they now do of the police". Too many citizens suffer from a near-total lack of knowledge about the police, the law and the courts system. For effective crime control, different segments of the criminal justice system—the police, prosecutors and the courts—must act in unison and not come in each other's way, as is happening now, helping the proliferation of crime. These is considerable strength in the argument that there has been an "over-judicialisation of the court process", and, in the name of safeguarding individual rights, the courts are granting bail even to confirmed criminals (who are subsequently repeating the crimes) and shirking away from deterrent punishment. Crime can be properly controlled only when there is vigorous law-enforcement and realistic punishment of the criminals. Referring to the crime situation in the UK, Sir Robert Mark has said in his book, *Policing a Perplexed Society,* that professional criminals are becoming aware of the limitations of the criminal justice system and discovering that professional cirme can be highly rewarding. According to him, in the UK a professinal robber or burglar has a six out of ten chance of acquittal. The odds are also in his favour in the USA In India, too, professional criminals backed by resourceful patrons are increasingly able to get the better of the criminal justice system. As John Alderson[14] says, "Too much is expected of our system of criminal justice which is capable of coping with some of the worst excesses, though in the main it disposes of mainly incompetent offenders". The press can highlight these infirmities of the criminal justice system and project accurately before the public the police point of view.

The press can also highlight serious police problems like appalling housing conditions, inadequate pay and allowances, long working hours and other constraints that plague the police organization. The stinging observation of the police commission of 1902 is valid even in to-day's context. "The police department, which intimately concerns the life of the people, has hitherto been starved.... and it is worthwhile to pay them the price required".

It is correctly said that a low rate of crime and a high rate of production are the two indicators of a healthy society. Freedom from crime and violence is one of the essential freedoms in a democratic society and the press can be of great help to the police in building a society not haunted by the spectre of rising crime. In India crime is rising (though the rate of increase is slower when compared to that of many Western countries) and from a realistic projection of contemporary trends one can expect a continued rise of crime and violence. It will be futile to expect that the police will be able to function effectively as "human agents of stability" in a turbulent and perplexed society unless the press also comes forward to sympathetically project the problems of law-enforcement, extend support to the police wherever needed and maintain the highest standards in reporting police news. But even when everything has been done to publicise the work of the police and enlist public interest and support, there will be a difference between shadow and substance unless each policeman by his conduct, attitude and performance enhances the image of the law enforcement agency in the public mind. Exemplary performance of basic and visible duties, along with better communication with the people through the press, will build up a fair, favourable and friendly image of the police on lasting foundations.

REFERENCES

1. Ben Whiteaker, *The Police in Society.*
2. Fifth report of the National Police Commission. Chap. XLI, p. 47.
3. Royal Commission on the Police (1962), Final Report.
4. *Encyclopaedia Britanni*, Vol. XI, "History of Publishing", p. 236.
5. Quoted in the article "No Comment-Law Enforcement and the Media" by Charles W. Steinmentz in *F.B.I. Law Enforcement Bulletin, July, 1979.*
6. Quotations are from the report of the Royal Commission on the Police.
8. Fifth Report of the National Police Commission.
9. Report of the Delhi Police Commission, Vol. I, p. 482.
10. *Crime Stoppers* by Demotria Martinez, *F.B.I. Law Enforcement Bulletin,* September, 1981.
11. Home Office Research Study No. 63.
12. Address of President Nixon at the graduation ceremony of the F.B.I. officers.
13. The quotation is from the book of Sir Robert Mark, *Policing a Perplexed Society.*
14. John Alderson: *"The Police We Deserve"*.

AppenDix

U.N. Standard Minimum Rules For The Treatment of Prisoners

Adopted by the First United Nations Congress on the Prevention of Crime and the Treatment of Offenders, held at Geneva in 1955, and approved by the Economic and Social Council by its resolutions 663 C (XXIV) of 31 July 1957 and 2076 (LXII) of 13 May 1977.

Preliminary Observations

1. The following rules are not intended to describe in detail a model system of penal institutions. They seek only, on the basis of the general consensus of contemporary thought and the essential elements of the most adequate systems of today, to set out what is generally haccepted as being good principle and practice in the treatment of prisoners and the management of institutions.

2. In view of the great variety of legal, social, economic and geographical conditions of the world, it is evident that not all of the rules are capable of application in all places and at all times. They should, however, serve to stimulate a constant endeavour to overcome practical difficulties in the way of their application, in the knowledge that they represent, as a whole, the minimum conditions which are accepted as suitable by the United Nationals.

3. On the other hand, the rules cover a field in which thought is constantly developing. They are not intended to preclude experiment and practices, provided these are in harmony with the principles and seek to further the purposes which derive from the text of the rules as a whole. It will always be justifiable for the central prison administration to authorize departures from the rules in this spirit.

4. (1) Part I of the rules covers the general management of institutions, and is applicable to all categories of prisoners, criminal or civil, untried or convicted, including prisoners subject to "security measures" or corrective measures ordered by the judge.

(2) Part II contains rules applicable only to the special categories dealt with in each section. Nevertheless, the rules under section A, applicable to prisoners under sentence, shall be equally applicable to

categories of prisoners dealt with in B,C and D, provided they do not conflict with the rules governing those categories and are for their benefit.

5. (1) The rules do not seek to regulate ιne management of institutions set aside for young persons such as Borstal Institutions or correctional schools, but in general Part I would be equallty applicable in such institutions.

(2) The category of young prisoners should include at atleast all young persons who come within the jurisdiction of juvenile courts. As a rule, such young persons should not be sentenced to imprisonment.

Part I
RULES OF GENERAL APPLICATION

Basic Principles

6. (1) The following rules shall be applied impartially. There shall be no discrimination on grounds of race, colour, sex, language, religion, political or other opinion, national or social origin, property, birth or other status.

(2) On the other hand, it is necessary to respect the religious beliefs and moral precepts of the group to which a prisoner belongs.

Register

7. (1) In every place where persons are imprisoned there shall be kept a bound registration book with numbered pages in which shall be entered in respect of each prisoner received:

(a) Information concerning his ldentity;

(b) The reasons for his commitment and the authority therefor;

(e) The day and hour of his admission and release.

(2) No person shall be received in an institution without a valid commitment order of which the details shall have been previously entered in the register.

Separation of categories.

8. The different categories of prisoners shall be kept in separate institutions or parts of institutions taking account of their sex, age, criminal record, the legal reason for their detention and the necessities of their treatment. Thus,

(a) Men and women shall so far as possible be detained in separate instititutions; in an institution which receives both men and women the whole of the premises allocated to women shall be entirely separate;

(b) Untried prisoners shall be kept separate from convicted prisoners;

(c) Persons imprisoned for debt and other civil prisoners shall be kept separate from persons imprisoned by reason of a criminal offence;

(d) Young prisoners shall be kept separate from adults.

Accommodation

9. (1) Where sleeping accommodation is in individual cells or rooms, each prisoner shall occupy by night a cell or room by himself. If for special reasons, such as temporary overcrowding, it becomes necessary for the central prison administration to make an exception to this rule, it is not desirable to have two prisoners in a cell or room.

(2) Where dormitories are used, they shall be occupied by prisoners carefully selected as being suitable to associate with one another in those conditions. There shall be regular supervision by night, in keeping with the nature of the institution.

10. All accommodation provided for the use of prisoners and in particular all sleeping accommodation shall meet all requirements of health, due regard being paid to climatic conditions and particularly to cubic content of air, minimum floor space, lighting, heating and ventilation.

11. In all places where prisoners are required to live or work.

(a) The windows shall be large enough to enable the prisoners to read or work by natural light, and shall be so constructed that they can allow the entrance of fresh air whether or not there is artificial ventilation;

(b) Artificial light shall be provided sufficient for the prisoners to read or work without injury to eyesight.

12. The sanitary installations shall be adequate to enable every prisoner to comply with the needs of nature when necessary and in a clean and decent manner.

13. Adequate bathing and shower installations shall be provided so that every prisoner may be enabled and required to have a bath or shower, at a temperature suitable to the climate, as frequently as necessary for general hygiene according to season and geographical region, but at least once a week in a temperate climate.

14. All parts of an institution regularly used by prisoners shall be properly maintained and kept scrupulously clean at all times.

Personal Hygiene

15. Prisoners shall be required to keep their persons clean, and to this end they shall be provided with water and with such toilet articles as are necessary for health and cleanliness.

16. In order that prisoners may maintain a good appearance compatible with their self-respect, facilities shall be provided for the proper care of the hair and beard, and men shall be enabled to shave regularly.

Clothing and Bedding

17 (1) Every prisoner who is not allowed to wear his own clothing shall be provided with an outfit of clothing suitable for the climate and adequate to keep him in good health. Such clothing shall in no manner be degrading or humiliating.

(2) All clothing shall be clean and kept in proper condition. Underclothing shall be changed and washed as often as necessary for the maintenance of hygiene.

(3) In exceptional circumstances, whenever a prisoner is removed outside the institution for an authorized purpose, he shall be allowed to wear his own clothing or other inconspicuous clothing.

18. If prisoners are allowed to wear their own clothing, arrangements shall be made on their admission to the institution. To ensure that it shall be clean and fit for use.

19. Every prisoner shall, in accordance with local or national standards, be provided with a separate bed, and with separate and sufficient bedding which shall be clean when issued, kept in good order and changed often enough to ensure its cleanliness.

Food

20. (1) Every prisoner shall be provided by the administration at the usual hours with food of nutritional value adequate for health and strength, of wholesome quality and well prepared and served.

(2) Drinking water shall be available to every prisoner whenever he needs it.

Exercise and Sport

21. (1) Every prisoner who is not employed in outdoor work shall have at least one hour of suitable exercise in the open air daily if the weather permits.

(2) Young prisoners, and others of suitable age and physique, shall receive physical and recreational training during the period of exercise. To this end, space, installations and equipment should be provided.

Medical Services

22. (1) At every institution there shall be available the services of at least one qualified medical officer who should have some knowledge of psychiatry. The medical services should be organized in close relationship to the general health administration of the community or nation. They shall include a psychiatric service for diagnosis and, in proper cases, the treatment of states of mental abnormality.

(2) Sick prisoners who require specialist treatment shall be transferred to specialized institutions or to civil hospitals. Where hospital facilities are provided in an institution, their equipment, furnishings and pharmaceutical supplies shall be proper for the medical care and treatment of sick prisoners, and there shall be a staff of suitable trained officers.

(3) The services of a qualified dental officer shall be available to every prisoner.

23. (1) In women's institutions there shall be special accommodation for all necessary pre-natal and post-natal care and treatment. Arrangements shall be made wherever practicable for children to be born in a hospital outside the institution. If a child is born in prison, this fact shall not be mentioned in the birth certificate.

(2) Where nursing infants are allowed to remain in the institution with their mothers, provision shall be made for a nursery staffed by qualified persons where the infants shall be placed when they are not in the care of their mothers.

24. The medical officer shall see and examine every prisoner as soon as possible after his admission and thereafter as necessary, with a view particularly to the discovery of physical or mental illness and the taking of all necessary measures; the segregation of prisoners suspected of infectious or contagious conditions; the noting of physical or mental defects which might hamper rehabilitation, and the determination of the physical capacity of every prisoner for work.

25. (1) The medical officer shall have the care of the physical and mental health of the prisoners and should daily see all sick prisoners, all who complain of illness, and any prisoner to whorm his attention is specially directed.

(2) The medical officer shall report to the director whenever he considers that a prisoner's physical or mental health has been or will be injuriously affected by continued imprisonment or by any condition of imprisonment.

26. (1) The medical officers shall regularly inspect and advise the director upon:

(a) The quantity, quality, preparation and service of food;

(b) The hygiene and cleanliness of the institution and the prisoners;

(c) The sanitation, heating, lighting and ventilation of the institution;

(d) The suitability and cleanliness of the prisoners' clothing and bedding;

(e) The observance of the rules concerning physical education and sports,

in cases where there is no technical personnel in charge of these activities.

(2) The director shall take into consideration the reports and advice that the medical officer submits according rule 25(2) and 26 and, in case he concurs with the recommendations made, shall take immediate steps to give effect to those recommendations; if they are not within his competence or if he does not concur with them, he shall immediately submit his own report and the advice of the medical officer to higher authority.

Discipline and Punishment

27. Discipline and order shall be maintained with firmness, but with not more restriction than is necessary for safe custody and well-ordered community life.

28. (1) No prisoner shall be employed, in the service of the institution, in any disciplinary capacity.

(2) This rule shall not, however, impede the proper functioning of systems based on self-government, under which specified social, educational or sports activities or responsibilities are entrusted, under supervision, to prisoners who are formed into groups for the purposes of treatment.

29. The following shall always be determined by the law or by the regulation of the competent administrative authority.

(a) Conduct constituting a disciplinary offence;

(b) The types and duration of punishment which may be inflicted;

(c) The authority competent to impose such punishment.

30. (1) No prisoner shall be punished except in accordance with the terms of such law or regulation, and never twice for the same offence.

(2) No prisoner shall be punished unless he has been informed of the offence alleged against him and given a proper opportunity of presenting his defence. The competent authority shall conduct a thorough examination of the case.

(3) Where necessary and practicable the prisoner shall be allowed to make his defence through an interpreter.

31. Corporal punishment, punishment by placing in dark cell, and all cruel, inhuman or degrading punishments shall be completely prohibited as punishments for disciplinary offences.

32. (1) Punishment by close confinement or reduction of diet shall never be inflicted unless the medical officer has examined the prisoner and certified in writing that he is fit to sustain it.

(2) The same shall apply to any other punishment that may be prejudicial to the physical or mental health of a prisoner. In no case may such punishment be contrary to or depart from the principle stated in Rule 31.

(3) The medical officer shall visit daily prisoners undergoing such punishments and shall advise the director if he considers the termination or alteration of the punishment necessary on grounds of physical or mental health.

Instruments of Restraint

33. Instruments of restraint, such as handcuffs, chains, irons and strait-jackets, shall never be applied as punishment. Furthermore, chains or irons shall not be used as restraints. Other instruments of restraint shall not be used except in the following circumstances:

(a) As a precaution against escape during a transfer, provide that they shall be removed when the prisoner appears before a judicial or administrative authority;
(b) On medical grounds by direction of the medical officer;
(c) By order of the director, if other methods of control fail, in order to prevent a prisoner from injuring himself or others or from damaging property; in such instances the director shall at once consult the medical officer and report to the higher administrative authoritdministrative authority;

34. The patterns and manner of use of instruments of restraint shall be decided by the central prison administration. Such instruments must not be applied for any longer time than in strictly necessary.

Information to and Complaints by Prisoners

35. (1) Every prisoner on admission shall be provided with written information about the regulations governing the treatment of prisoners of his category, the disciplinary requirements of the institution, the authorized methods of seeking information and making complaints,

and all such other matters as are necessary to enable him to understand both his rights and obligations and to adapt himself to the life of the institution.

(2) If a prisoner is illiterate, the aforesaid information shall be conveyed to him orally.

36. (1) Every prisoner shall have the opportunity each week day of making requests or complaints to the director of the institution or the officer authorized to represent him.

(2) It shall be possible to make requests or complaints to the inspector of prisons during his inspection. The prisoner shall have the opportunity to talk to the inspector or to any other inspecting officer without the director or other members of the staff being present.

(3) Every prisoner shall be allowed to make a request or complaint, without censorship as to substance but in proper form, to the central prison administration, the judicial authority or the other proper authorities through approved channels.

(4) Unless it is evidently frivolous or groundless, every request or complaint shall be promptly dealt with and replied to without undue delay.

Contact with the Outside World

37. Prisoners shall be allowed under necessary supervision to communicate with their family and reputable friends at regular intervals, both by correspondence and by received visits.

38. (1) Prisoners who are foreign nationals shall be allowed reasonable facilities to communicate with the diplomatic and consular representatives of the State to which they belong.

(2) Prisoners who are nationals of States without diplomatic or consular representation in the country and refugees or stateless persons shall be allowed similar facilities to communicate with the diplomatic representative of the State which takes charge of their interests or any national or international authority whose task it is to protect such persons.

39. Prisoners shall be kept informed regularly of the more important items of news by the reading of newspapers, periodicals or special institutional publications, by hearing wireless transmissions, by lectures or by any similar means as authorized or controlled by the administration.

Books

40. Every institution shall have a library for the use of all categories or prisoners, adequately stocked with both recreational and instructional books, and prisoners shall be encouraged to make full use of it.

Religion

41. (1) If the institution contains a sufficient number of prisoners of the same religion, a qualified representative of that religion shall be appointed or approved. If the number of prisoners justifies it and conditions permit, the arrangement should be on full-time basis.

(2) A qualified representative appointed or approved under paragraph (1) shall be allowed to hold regular services and to pay pastoral visits in private to prisoners of his religion at proper times.

(3) Access to a qualified representative of any religion shall not be refused to any prisoner. On the other hand, if any prisoner should object to a visit of any religious representative, his attitude shall be fully respected.

42. So far as practicable, every prisoner shall be allowed to satisfy the needs of his religious life by attending the services provided in the institution and having in his possession the books of religious observance and instruction of his denomination.

Retention of Prisoners' Property

43. (a) All money, valuables, clothing and other effects belonging to a prisoner which under the regulations of the institution he is not allowed to retain shall on his admission to the institution be placed in safe custody. An inventory thereof shall be signed by the prisoner. Steps shall be taken to keep them in good condition.

(2) On the release of the prisoner all such articles and money shall be returned to him except in so far as he has been authorized to spend money or send any such property out of the institution, or it has been found necessary on hygienic grounds to destroy any article of clothing. The prisoner shall sign a receipt for the articles and money returned to him.

(3) Any money or effects received for a prisoner from outside shall be treated in the same way.

(4) If a prisoner brings in any drugs or medicine, the medical officer shall decide what use shall be made of them.

Notification of Death, Illness and Transfer

44. (1) Upon the death or serious illness of, or serious injury to a

prisoner, or his removal to an institution for the treatment of mental affections, the director shall at once inform the spouse, if the prisoner is married, or the nearest relative and shall in any event inform any other person previously designated by the prisoner.

(2) A prisoner shall be informed at once of the death or serious illness of any near relative. In case of the critical illness of a near relative. the prisoner should be authorized, whenever circumstances allow, to go to his bedside either under escort or alone.

(3) Every prisoner shall have the right to inform at once his family of his imprisonment or his transfer to another institution.

Removal of Prisoners

45. (1) When the prisoners are being removed to or from an institution, they shall be exposed to public view as little as possible, and proper safeguards shall be adopted to protect them from insult, curiosity and publicity in any form.

(2) The transport of prisoners in conveyances with inadequate ventilation or light, or in any way which would subject them to unnecessary physical hardship, shall be prohibited.

(3) The transport of prisoners shall be carried out at the expense of the administration and equal conditions shall obtain for all of them.

Institutional Personnel

46. (1) The prison administration shall provide for the careful selection of every grade of the personnel, since it is on their integrity, humanity, professional capacity and personal suitability for the work that the proper administration of the institutions depends.

(2) The prison administration shall constantly seek to awaken and maintain in the minds both of the personnel and of the public the conviction that this work is a social service of great importance, and to this end all appropriate means of informing the public should be used.

(3) To secure the foregoing ends, personnel shall be appointed on a full-time basis as professional prison officers and have civil service status with security of tenure subject only to good conduct, efficiency and physical fitness. Salaries shall be adequate to attract and retain suitable men and women; employment benefits and conditions of service shall be favourable in view of the exacting nature of the work.

47. (1) The personnel shall possess an adequate standard of education and intelligence.

(2) Before entering on duty, the personnel shall be given a course of training in their general and specific duties and be required to pass theoretical and practical tests.

(3) After entering on duty and during their career, the personnel shall maintain and improve their knowledge and professional capacity by attending courses of inservice training to be organized at suitable intervals.

48. All members of the personnel shall at all times so conduct themselves and perform their duties as to influence the prisoners for good by their example and to command their respect.

49. (1) So far as possible, the personnel shall include a sufficient number of specialists such psychiatrists, psychologists, social workers, teachers and trade instructors.

(2) The services of social workers, teachers and trade instructors shall be secured on a permanent basis, without thereby excluding part-time or voluntary workers.

50. (1) The director of an institution should be adequately qualified for his task by character, administrative ability, suitable training and experience.

(2) He shall devote his entire time to his official duties and shall not be appointed on a part-time basis.

(3) He shall reside on the premises of the institution or in its immediate vicinity.

(4) When two or more institutions are under the authority of one director, he shall visit each of them at frequent intervals. A responsible resident official shall be in charge of each of these institutions.

51. (1) The director, his deputy, and the majority of the other personnel of the institution shall be able to speak the language of the greatest number of prisoners, or a language understood by the greatest number of them.

(2) Whenever necessary, the services of an interpreter shall be used.

52. (1) In an institution for both men and women, the part of the institution set aside for women shall be under the authourity of a responsible woman officer who shall have the custody of the keys of all that part of the institution.

(2) No male member of the staff shall enter the part of the institution set aside for women unless accompanied by a woman officer.

(3) Women prisoners shall be attended and supervised only by women officers. This does not, however, preclude male members of the

staff, particularly doctors and teachers, from carrying out their professional duties in institutions or parts of institutions set aside for women.

54. (1) Officers of the institutions shall not, in their relations with the prisoners, use force except in self-defence or in case of attempted escape, or active or passive physical resistance to an order based on law or regulations. Officers who have recouse to force must use no more than is strictly necessary and must report the incident immediately to the director of the institution.

(2) Prison officers shall be given special physical training to enable them to restrain aggressive prisoners.

(3) Except in special circumstances, staff performing duties which bring them into direct contact with prisoners should not be armed. Furthermore, staff should in no circumstances be provided with arms unless they have been trained in their use.

Inspection

55. There shall be a regular inspection of penal institutions and services by qualified and experienced inspectors appointed by a competent authority. Their task shall be in particular to ensure that these institutions are administered in accordance with existing laws and regulations and with a view to bringing about the objectives of penal and correctional services.

Part II
RULES APPLIABLE TO SPECIAL CATEGERIES

A. PRISONERS UNDER SENTENCE

Guiding Principles

56. The guiding principles hereafter are intended to show the spirit in which penal institutions should be administered and the purposes at which they should aim, in accordance with the declaration made under Preliminary Observation of the present text.

57. Imprisonment and other measures which result in cutting off an offender from the outside world are afflictive by the very fact of taking from the person the right of self-determination by depriving him of his liberty. Therefore the prison system shall not, except as incidental to justifiable segregation or the maintenance of discipline, aggravate the suffering inherent in such a situation.

58. The purpose and justification of a sentence of imprisonment or a similar measure derivative of liberty is ultimately to protect society

against crime. This end can only be achieved if the period of imprisonment is used to ensure, so far as possible, that upon his return to society the offender is not only willing but able to lead a law-abiding and self-supporting life.

59. To this end, the institution should utilize all the remedial educational, moral, spiritual and other forces and forms of assistance which are appropriate and available, and should seek to apply them according to the individual treatment needs of the prisoners.

60. (1) The regime of the institution should seek to minimize any differences between prison life and life at liberty which tend to lessen the responsibility of the prisoners or the respect due to their dignity as human beings.

(2) Before the completion of the sentence, it is desirable that the necessary steps be taken to ensure for the prisoner a gradual return to life in society. This aim may be achieved, depending on the case, by a pre-release regime organized in the same institution or in another appropriate institution, or by release on trial under some kind of supervision which must not be entrusted to the police but should be combined with effective social aid.

61. The treatment of prisoners should emphasize not their exclusion from the community, but their continuing part in it. Community agencies should, therefore, be enlisted wherever possible to assist the staff of the institution in the task of social rehabilitation of the prisoners. There should be in connection with every institution social workers charged with the duty of maintaining and improving all desirable relations of a prisoner with his family and with valuable social agencies. Steps should be taken to safeguard, to the maximum extent compatible with the law and the sentence, the rights relating to civil interests, social security rights and other social benefits of prisoners.

62. The medical services of the institution shall seek to detect and shall treat any physical or mental illness or defects which may hamper a prisoner's rehabilitation. All necessary medical, surgical and psychiatric services shall be provided to that end.

63. (1) The fulfilment of these principles requires individualization of treatment and for this purpose a flexible system of classifying prisoners in groups; it is therefore desirable that such groups should be distributed in separate institutions suitable for the treatment of each group.

(2) These institutions need not provide the same degree of security for every group. It is desirable to provide varying degrees of security

according to the needs of different groups. Open institutions, by the very fact that they provide no physical security against escape but rely on the self-discipline of the inmates, provide the conditions most favourable to rehabilitation for carefully selected prisoners.

(3) It is desirable that the number of prisoners in closed institutions should not be so large that the individualization of treatment is hindered. In some countries it is considered that the population of such institutions should not exceed five hundred. In open institutions the population should be as small as possible.

(4) On the other hand, it is undesirable to maintain prisons which are so small that proper facilities cannot be provided.

64. The duty of society does not end with a prisoner's release. There should, therefore, be governmental or private agencies capable of lending the released prisoner efficient after-care directed towards the lessening of prejudice against him and towards his social rehabilitation.

Treatment

65. The treatment of persons sentenced to imprisonment or a similar measure shall have as its purpose, so far as the length of the sentence permits, to establish in them the will to lead law-abiding and self-supporting lives after their release and to fit them to do so. The treatment shall be such as will encourage their self-respect and develop their sense of responsibility.

66. (1) To these ends, all appropriate means shall be used, including religious care in the countries where this is possible, education, vocational guidance and training, social casework, employment counselling, physical development and strengthening of moral character, in accordance with the individual needs of each prisoner, taking account of his social and criminal history, his physical and mental capacities and aptitudes, his personal temperament, the length of his sentence and his prospects after release.

(2) For every prisoner with a sentence of suitable length, the director shall receive, as soon as possible after his admission, full reports on all the matters referred to in the foregoing paragraph. Such reports shall always include a report by a medical officer, wherever possible qualified psychiatry, on the physical and mental condition of the prisoner.

(3) The reports and other relevant documents shall be placed in an individual file. This file shall be kept uptodate and classified in such a way that it can be consulted by the responsible personnel whenever the need arises.

Classification and Individualization

67. The purposes of classification shall be:

(a) To separate from others those prisoners who, by reason of their criminal records or bad characters, are likely to exercise a bad influence;

(b) To divide the prisoners into classes in order to facilitate their treatment with a view to their social rehabilitation.

68. So far as possible separate institutions or separate sections of an institution shall be used for the treatment of the different classes of prisoners.

69. As soon as posible after admission and after a study of the personality of each prisoner with a sentence of suitable length, a programme of treatment shall be prepared for him in the light of the knowledge obtained about his individual needs, his capacities and dispositions.

Privileges

70. Systems of privileges appropriate for the different classes of prisoners and the different methods of treatment shall be established at every institution, in order to encourage good conduct, develop a sense of responsibility and secure the interest and cooperation of the prisoners in their treatment.

Work

71. (1) Prison labour must not be of an afflictive nature.

(2) All prisoners under sentence shall be required to work, subject to their physical and mental fitness as determined by the medical officer.

(3) Sufficient work of a useful nature shall be provided to keep prisoners actively employed for a normal working day.

(4) So far as possible the work provided shall be such as will maintain or increase the prisoners' ability to earn an honest living after release.

(5) Vocational training in useful trades shall be provided for prisoners able to profit thereby and especialy for young prisoners.

(6) Within the limits compatible with proper vocational selection and with the requirements of institutional administration and discipline, the prisoners shall be able to choose the type of work they wish to perform.

72. (1) The organization and methods of work in the institutions shall resemble as closely as possible those of similar work outside institutions, so as to prepare prisoners for the conditions of normal occupational life.

(2) The interests of the prisoners and of their vocational training, however, must not be subordinated to the purpose of making a financial profit from an industry in the institution.

73. (1) Preferably institutional industries and farms should be operated directly by the administration and not by private contractors.

(2) Where prisoners are employed in work not controlled by the administration, they shall always be under the supervision of the institution's personnel. Unless the work is for other departments of the government the full normal wages for such work shall be paid to the administration by the persons to whom the labour is supplied, account being taken of the output of the prisoners.

74. (1) The precautions laid down to protect the safety and health of free workmen shall be equally observed ininstitutions.

(2) Provision shall be made to indemnify prisoners against industrial injury, including occupational disease, on terms not less favourable than those extended by law to free workmen.

75. (1) The maximum daily and weekly working hours of the prisoners shall be fixed by law or by administrative regulation, taking into account local rules of custom in regard to the employment of free workmen.

(2) The hours so fixed shall leave one rest day a week and sufficient time for education and other activities required as part of the treatment and rehabilitation of the prisoners.

76. (1) There shall be a system of equitable remuneration of the work of prisoners.

(2) Under the system prisoners shall be allowed to spend at least a part of their earnings on approved articles for their own use and to send a part of their earnings to their family.

(3) The system should also provide that a part of the earnings should be set aside by the administration so as to constitute a savings fund to be handed over to the prisoner on his release.

Education and Recreation

77. (1) Provision shall be made for the further education of all prisoners capable of profiting thereby including religious instruction in the countries where this is possible. The education of illiterates and young prisoners shall be compulsory and special attention shall be paid to it by the administration.

(2) So far as practicable, the education of prisoners shall be integrated with the educational system of the country so that after release they may continue their education without difficulty.

78. Recreational and cultural activities shall be provided in all institutions for the benefit of the mental and physical health of prisoners.

Social Relations and After-care

79. Special attention shall be paid to the maintenance and improvement of such relations between a prisoner and his family as are desirable in the best interests of both.

80. From the beginning of a prisoner's sentence consideration shall be given to his future after release and he shall be encouraged and assisted to maintain or establish such relations with persons or agencies outside the institution as may promote the best interests of his family and his own social rehabilitation.

81. (1) Services and agencies, governmental or otherwise, which assist released prisoners to re-establish themselves in society shall ensure, as far as possible and necessary, that released prisoners be provided with appropriate documents and identification papers, have suitable homes and work to go to, are suitably and adequately clothed having regard to the climate and season, and have sufficient means to reach their destination and maintain themselves in the period immediately following their release.

(2) The approved representatives of such agencies shall have all necessary access to the institution and to prisoners and shall be taken into consultation as to the future of a prisoner from the beginning of his sentence.

(2) It is desirable that the activities of such agencies shall be centralized or coordinated as far as possible in order to secure the best use of their efforts.

B. Insane and Mentally Abnormal Prisoners

82. (1) Persons who are found to be insane shall not be detained in prisons and arrangements shall be made to remove them to mental institutions as soon as possible.

(2) Prisoners who suffer from other mental diseases or abnormalities shall be observed and treated in specialized institutions under medical management.

(3) During their stay in a prison, such prisoners shall be placed under the special supervision of a medical officer.

(4) The medical or psychiatric service of the penal institutions shall provide for the psychiatric treatment of all other prisoners who are in need of such treatment.

83. It is desirable that steps should be taken, by arrangement with

the appropriate agencies, to ensure if necessary the continuation of psychiatric treatment after release and the provision of social-psychiatric after-care.

C. Prisoners Under Arrest or Awaiting Trial

84. (1) Persons arrested or imprisoned by reason of a criminal charge against them, who are detained either in police custody or in prison custody (jail) but have not yet been tried and sentenced, will be referred to as "untried prisoners" herein after in these rules.

(2) Uncohvicted prisoners are presumed to be innocent and shall be treated as such.

(3) Without prejudice to legal rules for the protection of individual liberty or prescribing the procedure to be observed in respect of untried prisoners, these prisoners shall benefit by a special regime which is described in the following rules in its essential requirements only.

85. (1) Untried prisoners shall be kept separate from convicted prisoners.

(2) Young untried prisoners shall be kept separate from adults and shall in principle be detained in separate institutions.

86. Untried prisoners shall sleep singly in separate rooms, with the reservation of different local custom in respect of the climate.

87. Within the limits compatible with the good order of the institution, untried prisoners may, if they so desire, have their food procured at their own expense from the outside either through the administration or through their family or friends. Otherwise, the administration shall provide their food.

88. (1) An untried prisoner shall be allowed to wear his own clothing if it is clean and suitable.

(2) If he wears prison dress, it shall be different from that supplied to convicted prisoners.

89. An untried prisoner shall always be offered opportunity to work, but shall not be required to work. If he chooses to work, he shall be paid for it.

90. An untried prisoner shall be allowed to procure at his own expense or at the expense of a third party such books, newspapers, writing materials and other means of occupation as are compatible with the interests of the administration of justice and the security and good order of the institution.

91. An untried prisoner shall be allowed to be visited and treated by his own doctor or dentist if there is reasonable ground for his application and he is able to pay any expenses incurred.

92. An untried prisoner shall be allowed to inform immediately his family of his detention and shall be given all reasonable facilities for communicating with his family and friends, and for receaiving visits from them, subject only to restrictions and supervision as are necessary in the interests of the administration of justice and of the security and good order of the institution.

93. For the purpose of his defence, an untried prisoner shall be allowed to apply for free legal aid where such aid is available, and to receive visits from his legal adviser with a view to his defence and to prepare and hand to him confidential instructions. For these purposes, he shall if he so desired be supplied with writing material. Interviews between the prisoner and his legal adviser may be within sight but not within the hearing of a police or institution official.

D. Civil Prisoners

94. In countries where the law permits imprisonment for debt, or by order of a court under any other non-criminal process, persons so imprisoned shall not be subjected to any greater restriction or severity than is necessary to ensure safe custody and good order. Their treatment shall be not less favourable than that of untried prisoners, with the reservation, however, that they many possibly be required to work.

Index